Cheryl Malkowski

doodle QUILTING

Over 120 Continuous-Line Machine-Quilting Designs

PUBLISHER:
Amy Marson

CREATIVE DIRECTOR:
Gailen Runge

ART DIRECTOR:
Kristy Zacharias

EDITOR:
Liz Aneloski

TECHNICAL EDITOR:
Helen Frost

COVER/BOOK DESIGNER:
April Mostek

PRODUCTION COORDINATOR:
Zinnia Heinzmann

PRODUCTION EDITOR:
S. Michele Fry

ILLUSTRATOR:
Cheryl Malkowski

PHOTOGRAPHY by Christina Carty-Francis and Diane Pedersen of C&T Publishing, Inc., unless otherwise noted

Published by C&T Publishing, Inc., P.O. Box 1456, Lafayette, CA 94549

Library of Congress Cataloging-in-Publication Data

Malkowski, Cheryl, 1955-

Doodle quilting : over 120 continuous-line machine-quilting designs / Cheryl Malkowski.

p. cm.

ISBN 978-1-60705-636-2 (soft cover)

1. Machine quilting--Patterns. I. Title.

TT835.M27175 2012

746.46--dc23

2012015425

Printed in China

10 9 8 7 6 5 4 3 2 1

contents

introduction

On any given day, most quilters have at least one quilt top that is begging to be quilted. These are not necessarily masterpieces or competition quilts, but quilts for family, friends, or even a local charity. They don't call for intricate, precise patterns, but some sort of allover design to hold the quilt together. These are my favorites to quilt—quilts that are really all about the fabric; the stitching adds a bonus layer of interest. My theory is that these quilts should have interesting quilting patterns, even if they don't require them. Patterns draw viewers closer to the quilt and invite them to really explore it.

But what I hear from quilters is, "I'm not at all artistic!" or "I could never do that!"

In my prequilting days as a preschool classroom assistant, I taught representational drawing to a group of four- and five-year-olds. The children were fabulous. By the end of the unit, they were drawing a rose in a vase on a table with a table runner, and it looked like the real thing. These were not genius four- and five-year-olds; it's just that the thought had never occurred to them that they couldn't draw. So they just did it. They drew the rose still life by breaking down the picture into understandable shapes and drawing each shape one at a time.

Now, I know that you, my fellow quilters, have, at the very least, the artistic abilities of a young child, but you probably have been telling yourself since you were about nine years old that you can't draw, because your simple drawings didn't meet the standards of your sophisticated minds. Now you probably look at a subject or design and decide you can't draw it, so you don't even try. But maybe your drawings never advanced after elementary school because nobody ever broke down the simple shapes for you.

The principles that worked for my preschool class will work for quilters looking for designs to put on quilts. Granted, you are going to need to master the actual machine-quilting process, but the hardest part of quilting is deciding where you are going to stitch next. We will discuss that decision in this book as you learn about breaking down simple shapes, traveling shapes, and shapes that stay put—or "boomerangs" as I call them. Learning how to draw simple shapes and then putting them together to make a quilting design is the first step toward more interesting quilting, because you have to know how the design behaves and how to draw it before you can quilt it. So let's get to it!

how to use THIS BOOK

The goal of this book is to help you gain confidence with the basic shapes that comprise most quilt designs. Knowing the characteristics of individual motifs, how they work, and how they work together is what every quilter needs to know to get beyond stitching in-the-ditch.

To make this easy, I've prepared some drawing exercises—well, actually, motifs to trace—so you can get the idea of where you're going. This book has a special lie-flat binding that will make tracing easier. Turn the book so the pages are in the landscape format. Use Quilter's Vinyl, available at quilt shops and from C&T Publishing, and a low-odor, fine-point, dry-erase marker. The vinyl can be used over and over with these markers. Dry-erase markers can be found at office supply stores or even the office supply section of a department store. You should be able to find a package of multiple markers for less than $5.

Once your lines are smooth while tracing and you see where you're going, try holding the pen in your fist or with your hand farther up from the point. This will keep your elbow off the table and force you to draw with your whole arm. Tracing this way more closely resembles the movement necessary to machine quilt, whether on a domestic or a longarm machine.

Take it one step further by using another pen or pencil and a rubber band or hair elastic to make a cross-piece. Try tracing this way. Your dominant hand will lead, and you will get used to the feeling of moving both hands together.

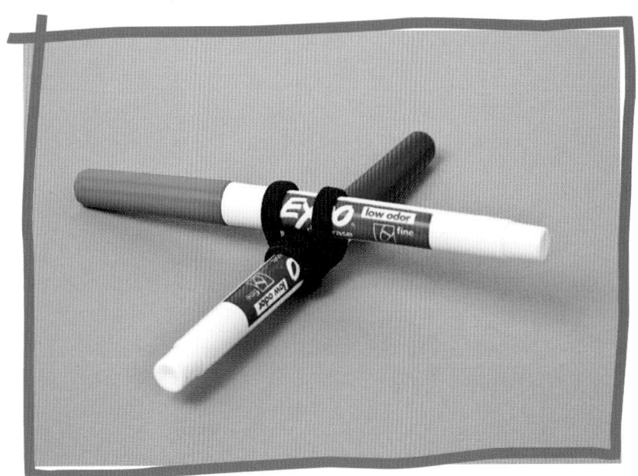

Then practice the motif without tracing. Mix different motifs together and fill up the Quilter's Vinyl. Erase and do it again! Doodle at every opportunity, and doodle with purpose, keeping your pen on the paper, so that you're not starting and stopping.

When you have a good idea of how your motifs will work together, you will be closer to success when you actually start stitching. Go to the sewing machine and start a new adventure! Need a moment to figure out where to go next? Just put your needle down and think for a bit, then continue to doodle with your machine.

travelers

**trav•el•er (noun) [trá və lər, tráv' lər]—
one who journeys to a specific place**

Traveler motifs can stand alone as an allover design, or they can be used in combination with other motifs. Every allover quilt design needs to include at least one traveler because they are the elements that make a design work.

Most commonly, I use a plain vine, loops, or echoing in my allover design because they can get me out of jams. For example, if I am quilting away in the lower right section of the area and see that I've inadvertently left a section unquilted in the upper left section, I need a way to get back there. By including a traveler in my repertoire of motifs, I can do just that—travel back to where I need to fill in. We'll look at that scenario more closely in the Ensembles chapter (page 58). For now, let's practice the basics!

Loops

Easy enough—they're primary-school, cursive lowercase E's!

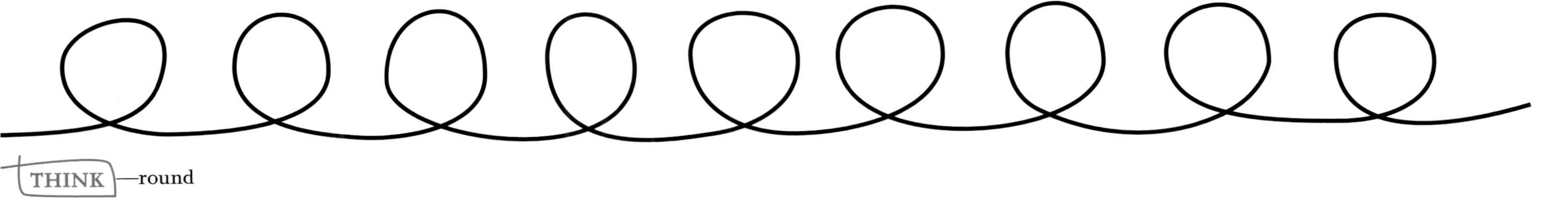

THINK—round

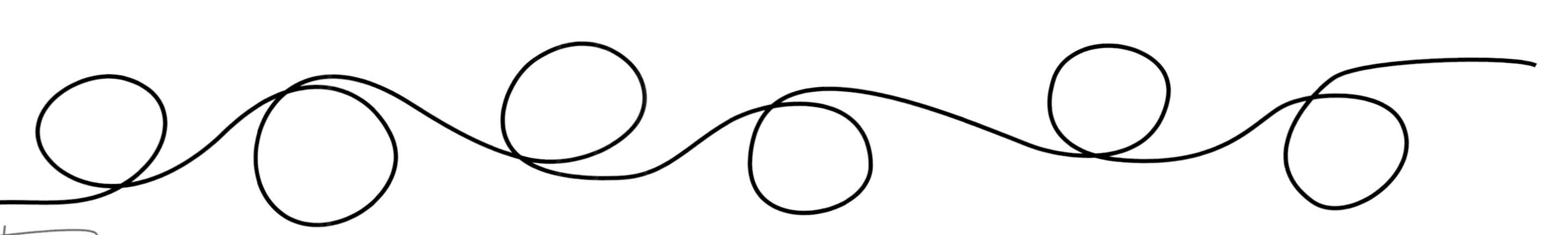

THINK—up and round and down and round

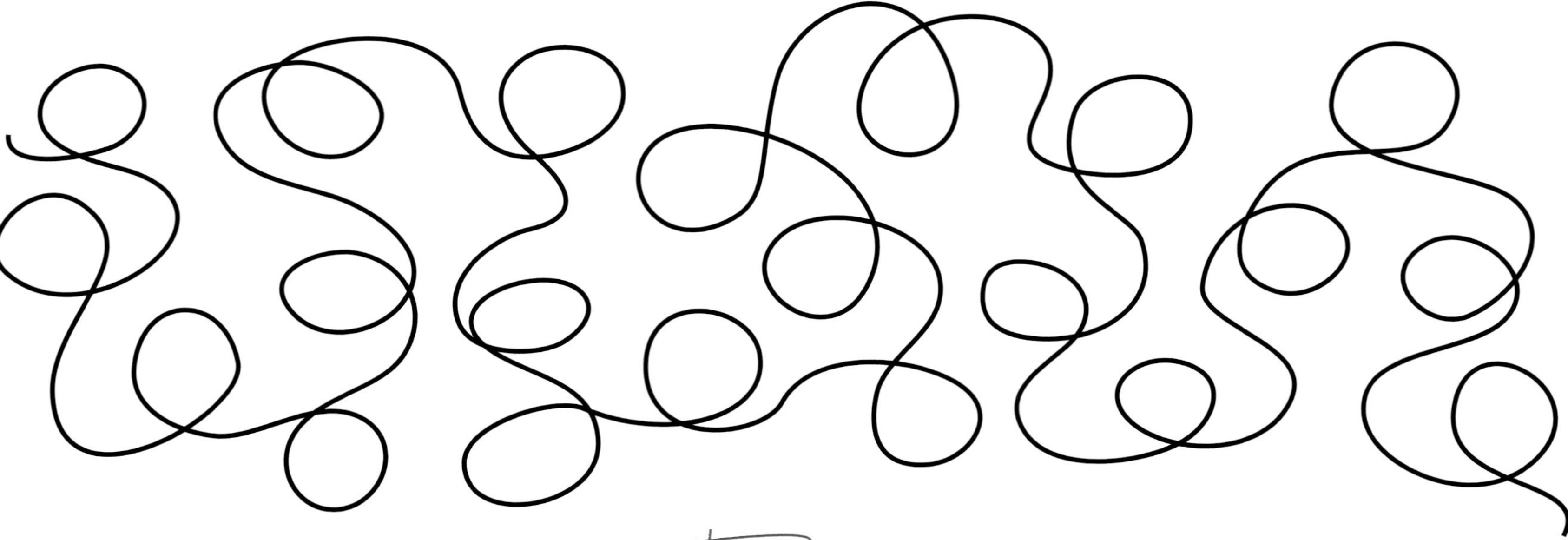

Now add a vine—a curvy line—between loops. To fill in the space, THINK—round and curve and round and curve.

How about a double loop? Just go around twice, when there is room.

TRAVELING CIRCLES

These circles are great for dividing a space or filling in feather stems. Make a circle and go around another half circle before beginning the next one. Keep the circles right next to each other.

THINK—around and a half and around and a half …

PEBBLES

Vary the size, as I did, or keep the size consistent. Go around each circle at least twice. Lines don't need to be precisely on top of each other, but they should be close, and circles should be tightly spaced.

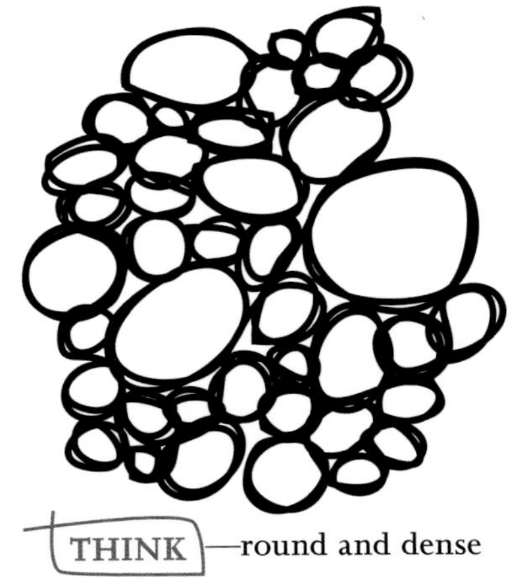

THINK—round and dense

CURSIVE LOWERCASE E'S AND L'S

These are great for small borders! If you have small blocks along the border, use these motifs to keep your spacing consistent by putting all your L's at a seam and all the E's in between.

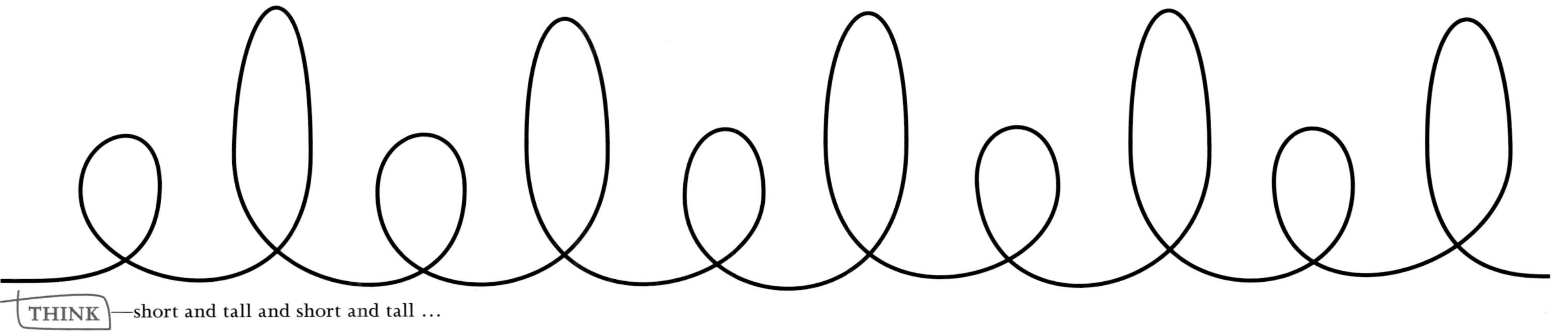

THINK—short and tall and short and tall …

C's or Scrolls

Use these for small borders or allover fills.

Begin with a backward C. Pivot and follow around the outside of the C back to the side where you began. When you touch the bottom of the first C, reverse direction, still on the outside, and go to the opposite side to begin the next C. Repeat.

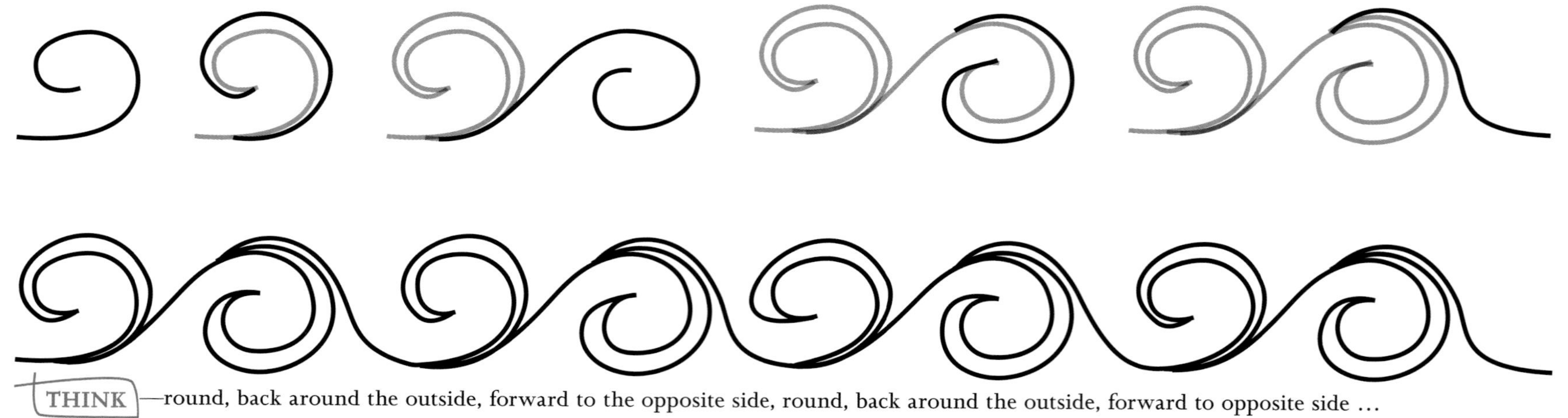

THINK—round, back around the outside, forward to the opposite side, round, back around the outside, forward to opposite side …

The retracing of the C can follow the original path for a tighter scroll. Think the same as before, only retrace on top of the C instead of next to it.

When using this for an allover fill, you can use either open or closed C's. Make the C, retrace back to the opposite side, and then go off in a different direction for the next C. The C's can be evenly or randomly sized.

Flames

Flames are a fast and easy allover pattern. The key to successful Flames is to constantly vary the length of each curvy line (vine) and frequently change the direction you turn after the point. So if you go to the right once or twice, then try going to the left to fill any empty space. You must decide ahead of time how far apart you want to space your Flames, so you can fill in accordingly.

THINK—medium vine (or curvy line), point, to the left short, point, to the left long, point, to the right short . . .

Bark

Bark is Flames (page 16) with round tips instead of points. If you turn the motif horizontal, it makes a different kind of water. Use the same rules as for Flames.

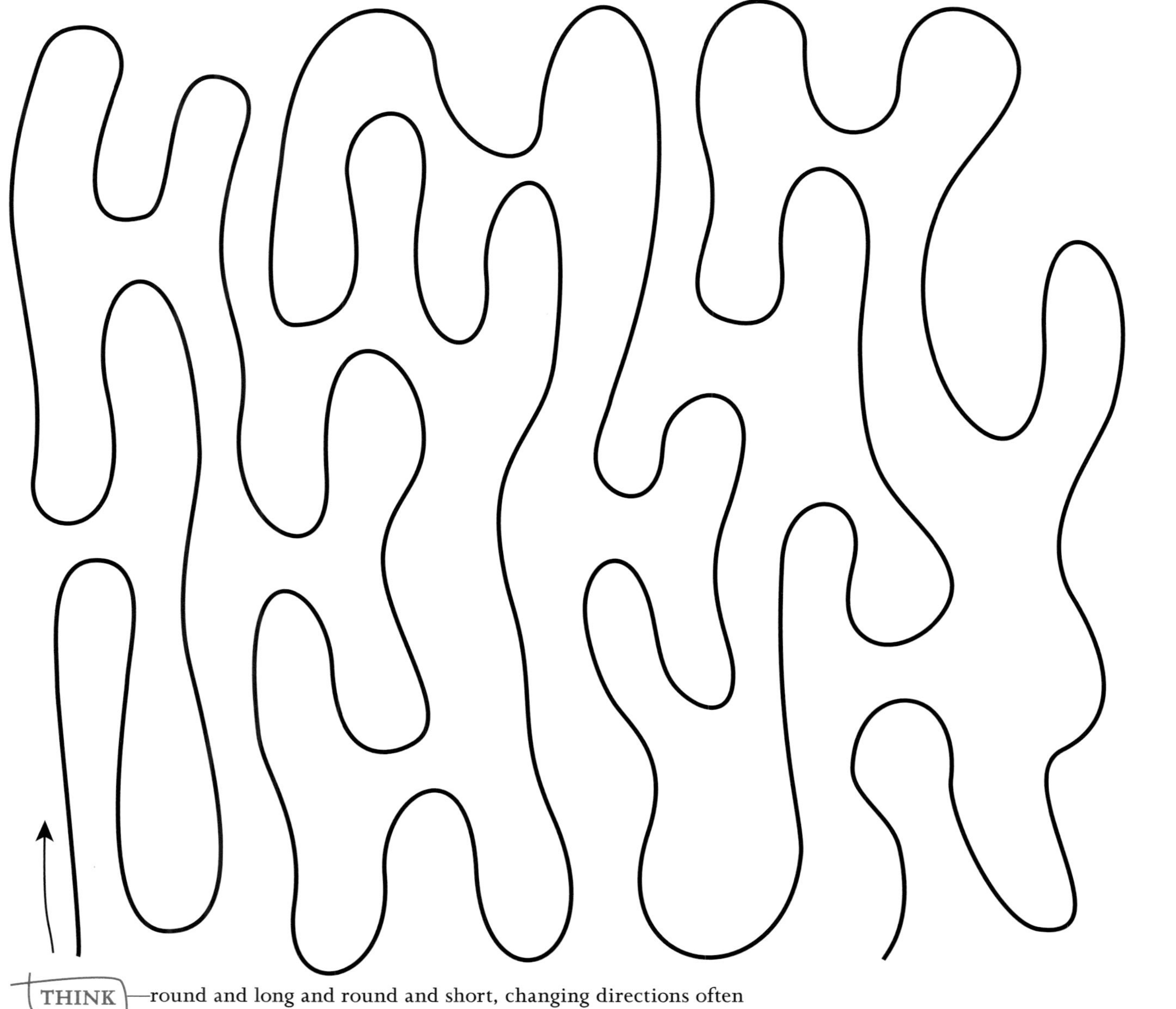

THINK—round and long and round and short, changing directions often

Echoing

Echoing is usually used around an appliqué shape, such as this flower. It's simple because you always know where you're going. Determine ahead of time how far apart you want the echoes to be, and then go directly around the edge of the motif—the line doesn't show here—and spiral outward, using the previous line as a guide.

Think about spacing and following the path.

There is no rule that says your echo has to be smooth and exactly match the contour of the shape. You can use a whimsical, wavy line, which is especially useful for beginners because it doesn't look like you're trying to match anything. Think about spacing and keeping the lines from touching.

Sometimes you may just want to scribble around the edge of a shape, which can be useful for nailing down raw-edged appliqué.

THINK—"This is my quilt, and I can do what I want."

Teeth

This shape is helpful when making flowers. It looks like a molar to me.

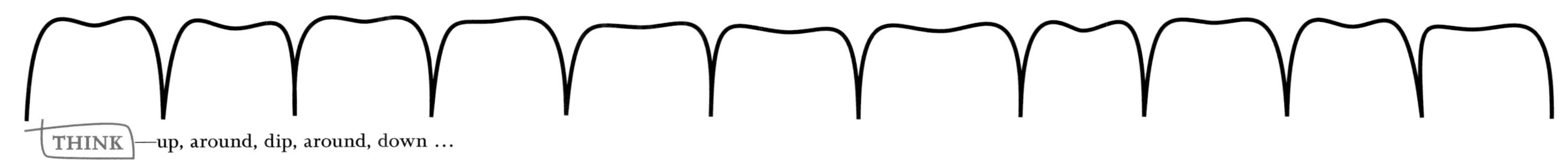

THINK—up, around, dip, around, down …

Spikeys

Add excitement between curved motifs!

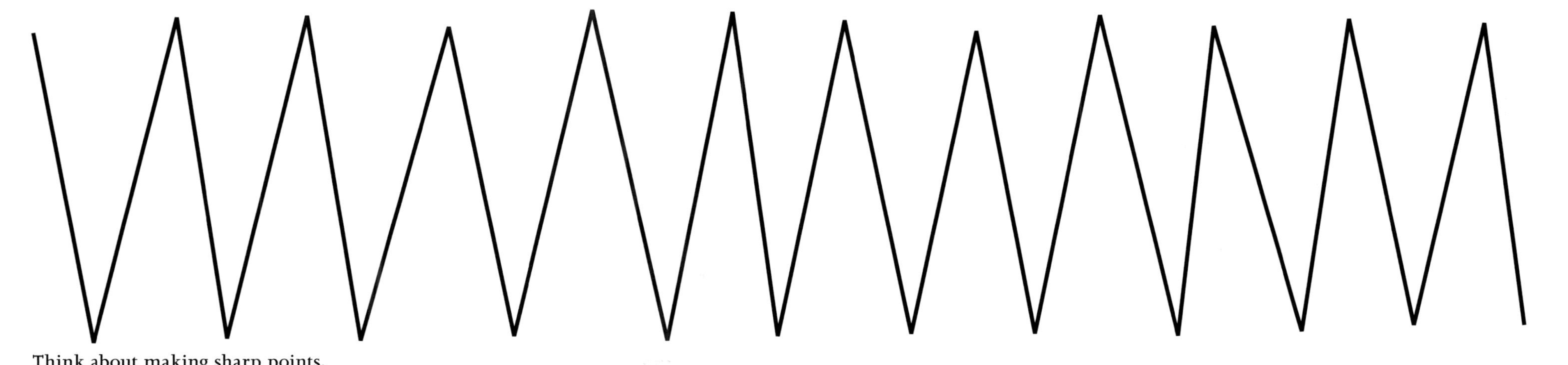

Think about making sharp points.

Sunshines

These are like Spikeys, but they're curved. They make great flowers.

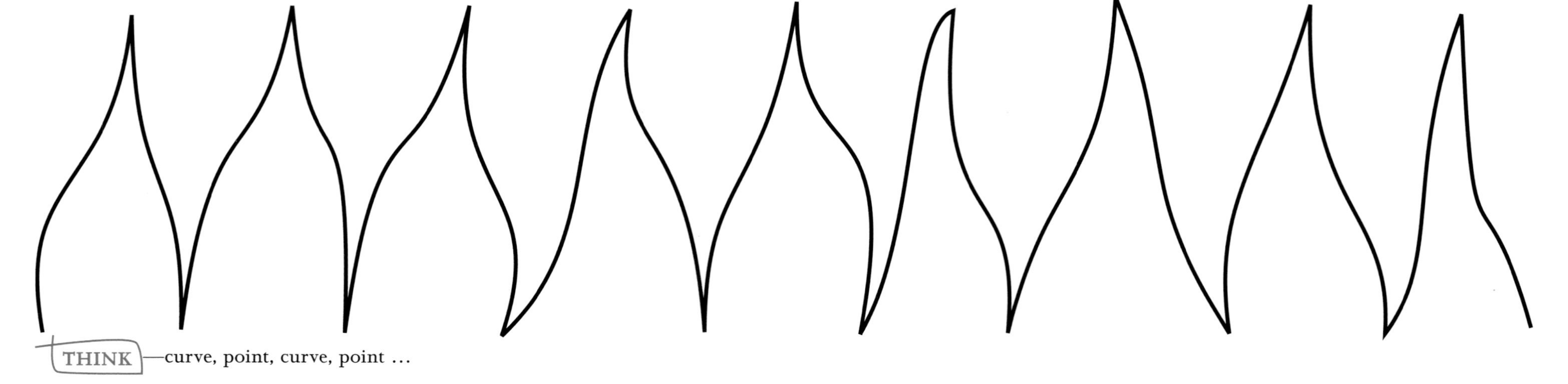

THINK—curve, point, curve, point …

Flower Petals

A row of simple arcs, this motif can be used for petals or clamshell designs.

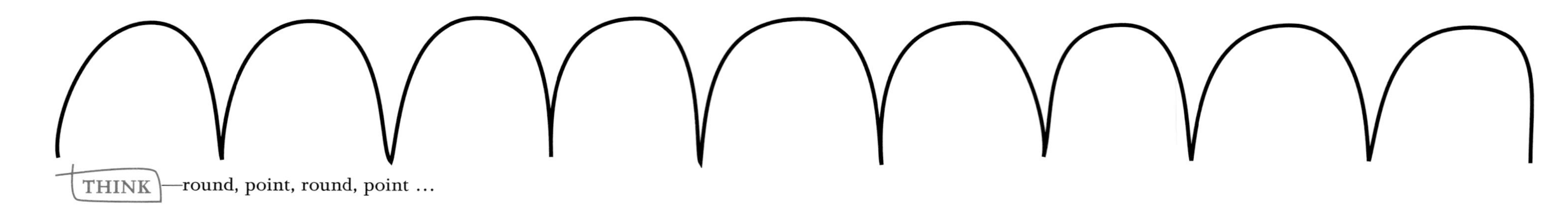

THINK—round, point, round, point …

Water

CALM WATER

There is not much motion in this ocean. This motif can be as relaxed as you can smoothly draw it.

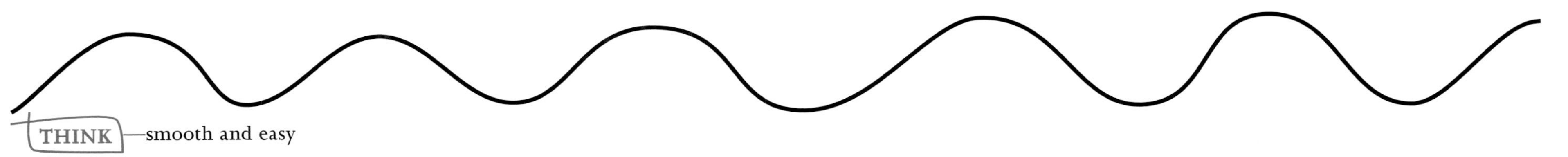

THINK—smooth and easy

WAVY CHECKS

Calm Water going both horizontally and vertically makes Wavy Checks, an easy allover pattern. Decide how far apart you want your lines to be, and then make a line of Calm Water across the area you want to fill. Follow the edge of the quilt or the seamline of the area down the predetermined length. Make another line of Calm Water back to the other side. Repeat until your vertical area is filled. Then go to the bottom of the area and, keeping on the outside, go back a predetermined distance. Start with more Calm Water to make a vertical line; then go over and down until the area is filled.

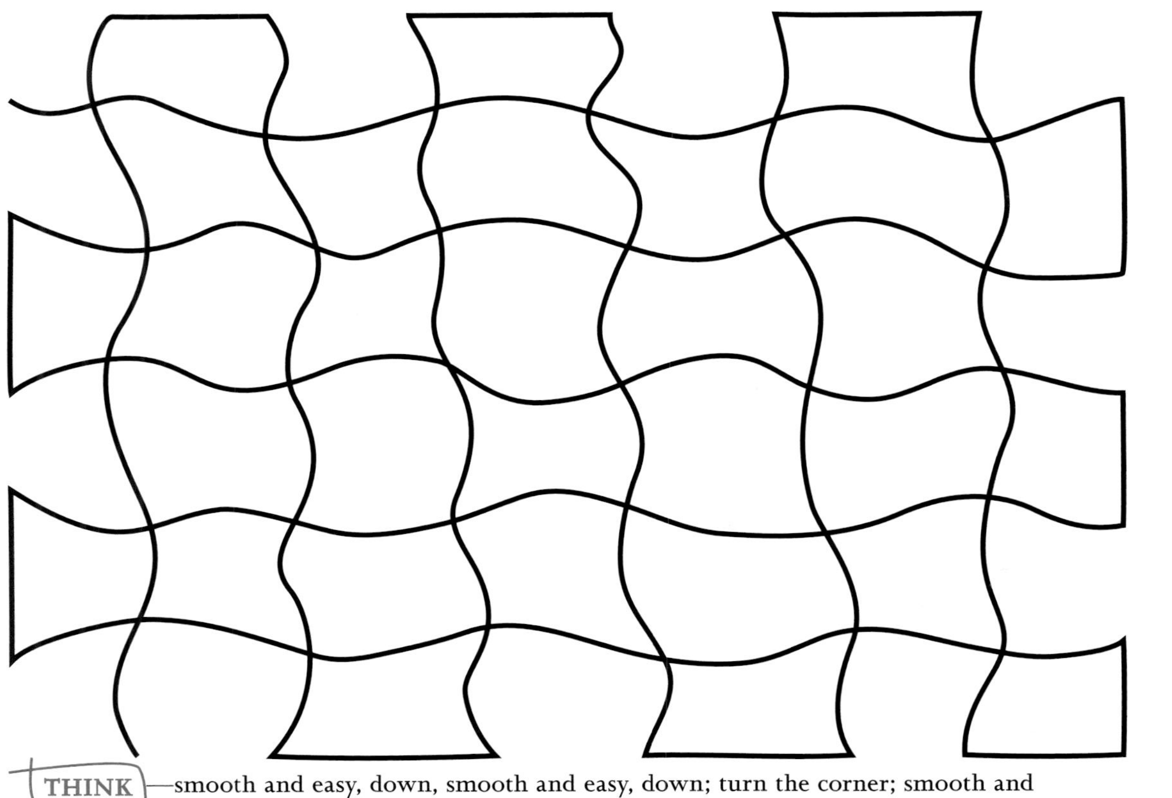

THINK—smooth and easy, down, smooth and easy, down; turn the corner; smooth and easy, over, smooth and easy, over …

CALM WITH WAVES

Add an occasional wave to Calm Water and you have the perfect motif for an aquarium or fish-themed quilt. Don't be tempted to add too many waves—a few will do. Waves can point up or down.

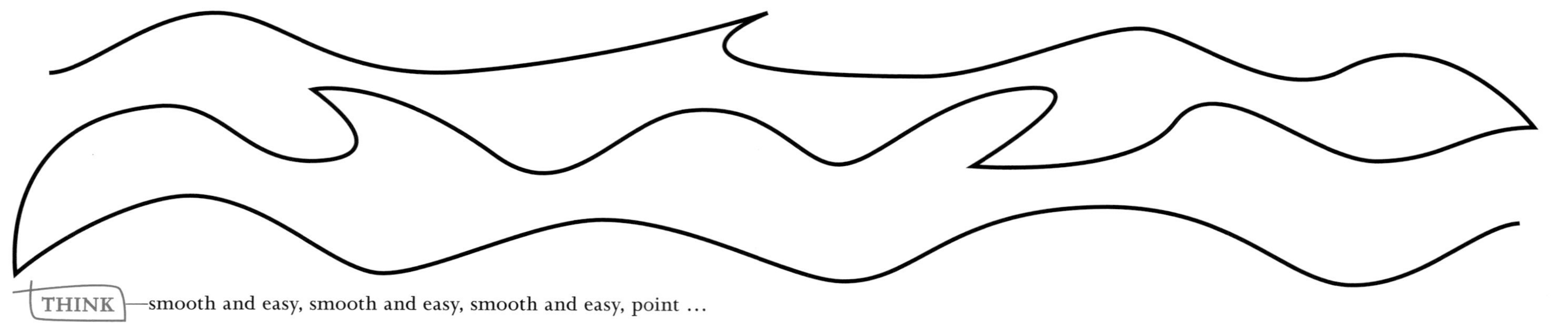

THINK—smooth and easy, smooth and easy, smooth and easy, point …

EXCITED WATER

Make more ripples, closer together.

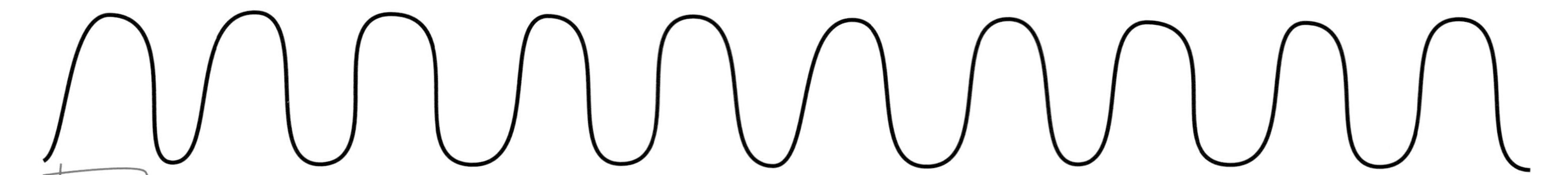

THINK—up and round and down and round …

MEANDERING OR STIPPLING

Basically, this is Excited Water gone awry. The curves are closer together, and you have to remember to change direction frequently. If you're a beginner, try making no more than two bumps in the same direction, which is easiest when you fill in the bottom of the area first and work backward. That way you can see where you need to go next.

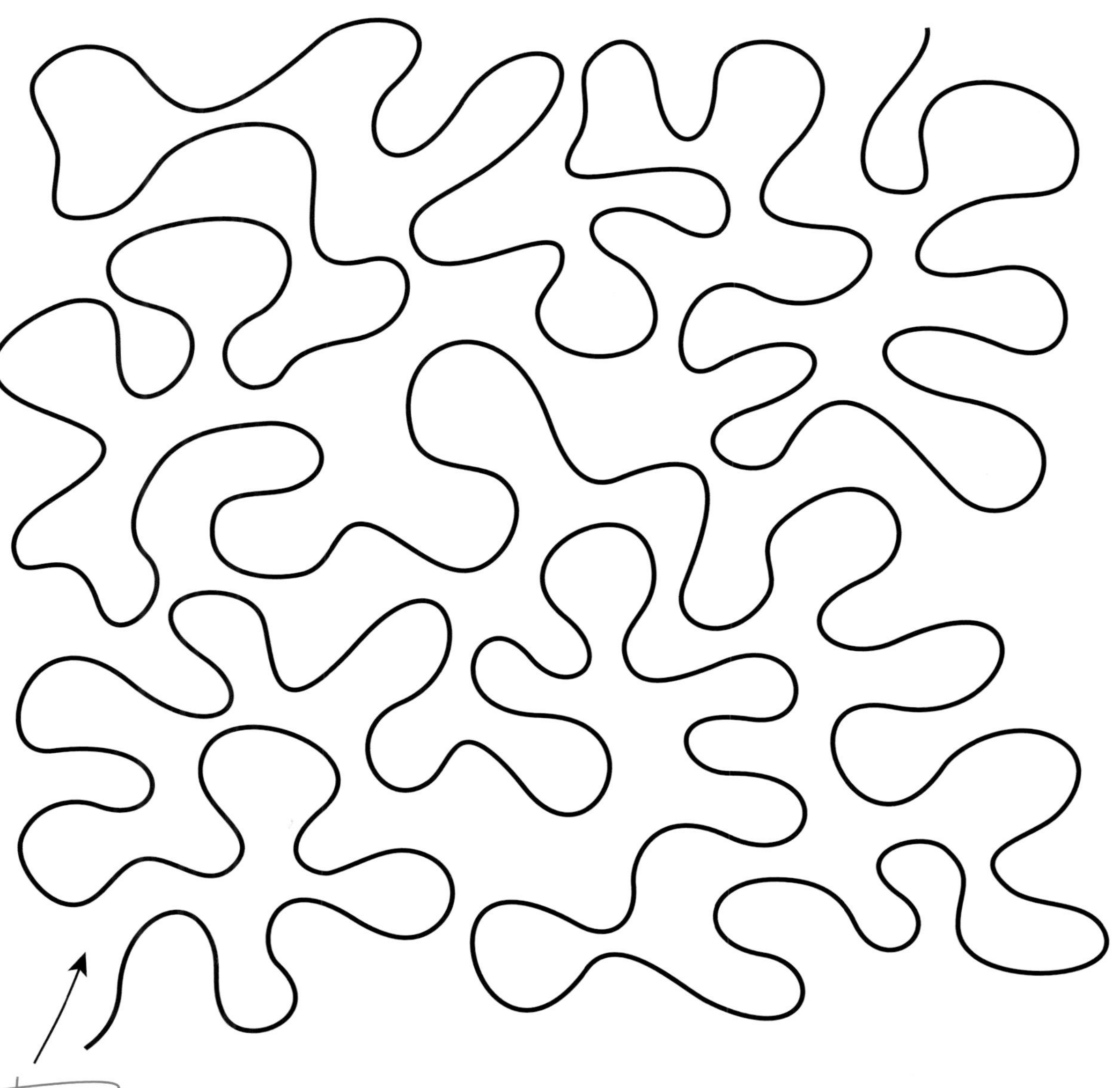

THINK—round and round and change direction …

Hooks (Question Marks)

Sometimes called a Question Mark or Finger Feathers, the Hook is a shape you will use over and over, so practice it from right to left and left to right, upside down and backward! The dotted lines are there for your imaginary stems.

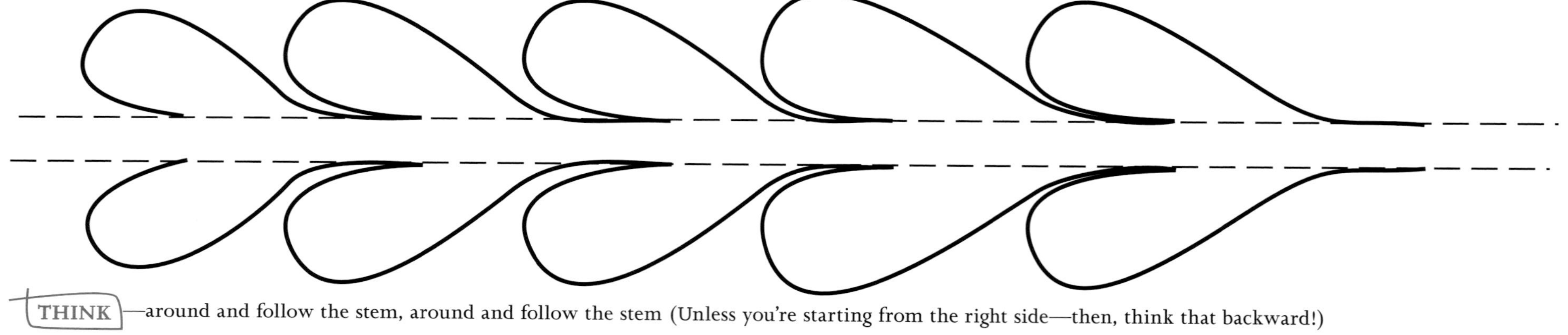

THINK—around and follow the stem, around and follow the stem (Unless you're starting from the right side—then, think that backward!)

DOUBLE-HOOK GARLAND

You may not use these in a row like this, but if you do and you space them so they kiss, you've got a pretty fancy feather! Start at the star, which is the bottom of the question mark, then come to the point, and echo back around the outside to where you started.

THINK—question mark, outside echo, question mark, outside echo ...

Swirlies

ROUND SWIRLIES

The key to a successful Swirly is to determine ahead of time how far apart you want the lines. Let's say you want ½″ spacing. When you make the first spiral, start from the outside and work your way in, leaving 1″ between lines, so that when you come back out, your spacing is right. With any of the Swirlies, you can make a point or a rounded line when you get to the center and reverse direction.

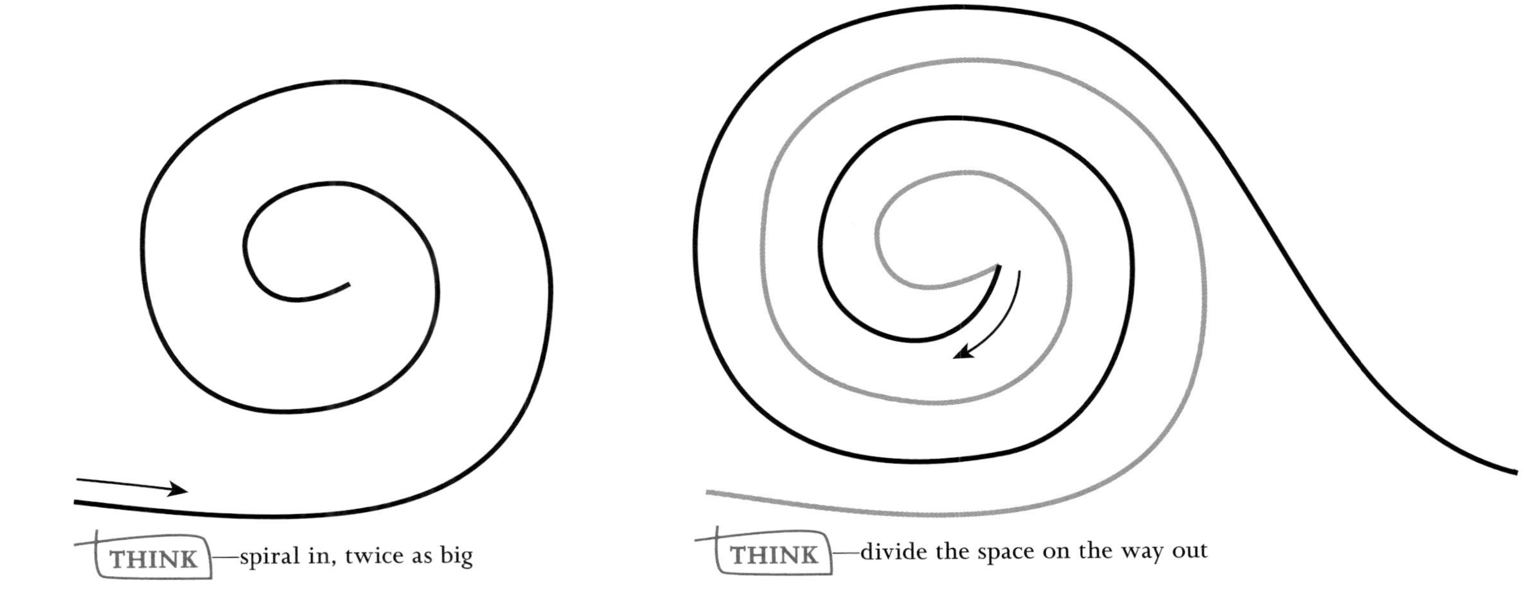

THINK—spiral in, twice as big

THINK—divide the space on the way out

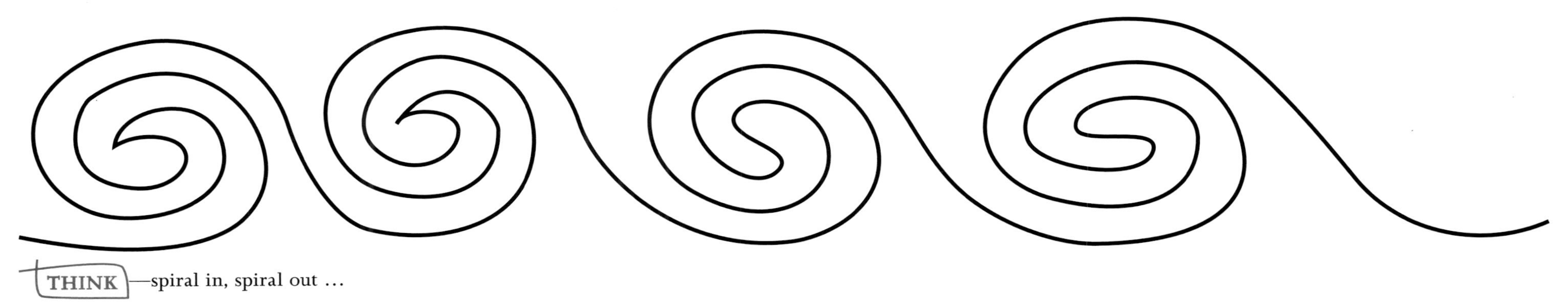

THINK—spiral in, spiral out …

SQUARE SWIRLIES, OR TECHNICALLY, GREEK KEYS

The trick here is to get the third vertical line to be three times as long as your desired spacing above the bottom horizontal line, so that you have room to turn around.

Think about spacing and crisp corners.

TRIANGLE SWIRLIES

I cannot guarantee that this will ever be a shape you can do without strenuous thinking; it's never been easy for me, but I love how it looks! It's the same principle as in Square Swirlies (page 26), but with three sides.

Think about spacing and crisp corners.

TEARDROP 1-2-3

This is one of my favorite motifs, and so easy!

There is a secret to this that nobody told me, but I'm going to tell you now: It makes a difference which way you start this motif. You generally make three concentric Teardrops, reversing direction each time, so you finish an individual motif on the same side of the motif as you finish the first Teardrop, as shown. You can make a vine by alternating directions each time you start a new Teardrop 1-2-3.

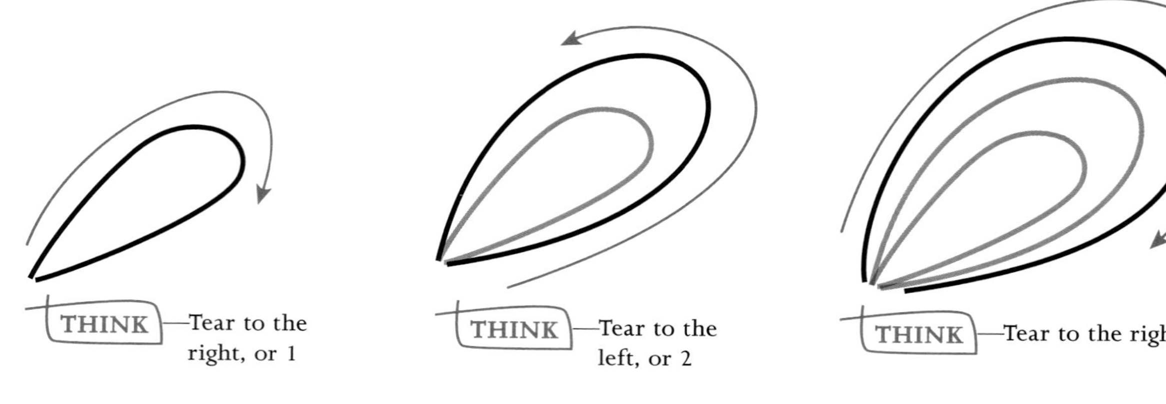

Teardrop 1-2-3 Vine

The goal is to return all three concentric Teardrops to the same starting point. Sometimes that will not be possible, so you will need to bounce off a neighbor.

Teardrop 1-2-3 Allover

For an allover pattern, use your knowledge of where each motif is going so you can fill all the space. Sometimes you'll need to go to a certain place and will have to use a lot of right-2-3's in a row. That's okay! You'll get used to thinking before you start each motif. The worst-case scenario? You may have to do a 1-2-3-4 to get where you need to go.

When practicing, start at the star and stop at the dot. The points are intentionally left farther apart than normal to make it easier to follow the lines.

THINK—1-2-3 and be aware of where you need to fill in.

boomerangs

boo•mer•ang (noun) [bóo mə rang]—a device that, when used properly, returns to the point of origin

Thank you for shopping at Amazon.co.uk!

5 C4

Invoice for
Your order of 9. November 2012
Order ID 203-8664715-1742743
Invoice number EUVINS1-OFS-DE-73841454
Invoice date 7. January 2013

Billing Address
Christine Brady
35 West Park
Carnock
Dunfermline, Fife KY12 9JU
United Kingdom

Shipping Address
Christine Brady
35 West Park
Carnock
Dunfermline, Fife KY12 9JU
United Kingdom

Qty.	Item	Our Price (excl. VAT)	VAT Rate	Total Price
1	**Doodle Quilting: Over 120 Continuous-Line Machine-Quilting Designs** Paperback. Malkowski, Cheryl. 1607056364 (** P-1-P123E542 **)	£14.07	0%	£14.07
	Shipping charges	£0.00		£0.00
	Subtotal (excl. VAT) 0%			£14.07
	Total VAT			£0.00
	Total			£14.07

Conversion rate - £1.00 : £1.00

This shipment completes your order.

You can always check the status of your orders or change your account details from the "Your Account" link at the top of each page on our site.

Thinking of returning an item? PLEASE USE OUR ON-LINE RETURNS SUPPORT CENTRE.

Our Returns Support Centre (www.amazon.co.uk/returns-support) will guide you through our Returns Policy and provide you with a printable personalised return label. Please have your order number ready (you can find it next to your order summary, above). Our Returns Policy does not affect your statutory rights.

Amazon EU S.a.r.L, 5 Rue Plaetis, L-2338, Luxembourg
VAT number : GB727255821

Please note - this is not a returns address - for returns - please see above for details of our online returns centre

0/DclGnbGWR/-1 of 1-//DOM_UK/econ-uk/5656855/0108-22:45/0108-10:33 Pack Type : C4

Leaves

The great thing about nature motifs is that they don't have to be perfect. Shapes in nature are notoriously imperfect but consistently similar. It is all about giving the impression of the motif.

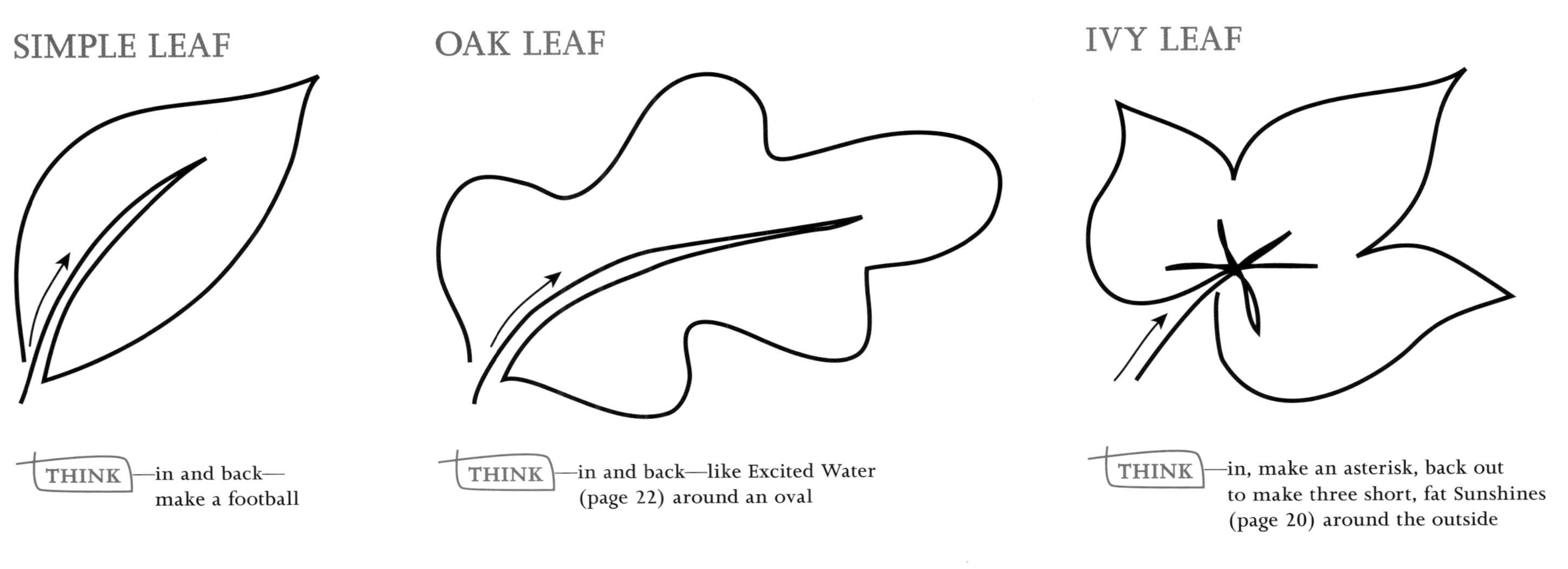

MAPLE LEAF

For some leaves, starting with a more complex inner-vein structure makes drawing the outer leaf shape easier. The Maple Leaf is one such leaf.

Go in to the far end of the vein, and then backtrack along that vein, shooting out and back to the center vein with each side vein as needed for the leaf shape.

THINK—in, back a bit, out and return, out and return, back a bit, out and return, out and return, back down the stem

THINK—points outward and deep dips between veins

JAGGED-EDGE LEAF

This is another leaf that is easier when started with an inner-vein structure. The general leaf shape is a football, like the Simple Leaf, but at intervals there are short, sharp lines that jut back toward the leaf base and that roughly parallel the angles of the upward-curving veins.

THINK—in, back a bit, out and return, back a bit, out and return—until the veins are complete. Then think about the overall shape as having little juts that point toward the leaf base.

GINKGO LEAF

Ginkgo leaves are fan shaped, with an irregular toothlike outer edge. All the veins radiate from the base of the leaf. They're shown here with Loose Cluster Berries (page 34).

THINK—curve out from the stem, arc around with wavy teeth, curve back to the stem, and then in and back, in and back, in and back for the veins

HOLLY

It helps me to imagine a football shape before I start Holly leaves, so I've added one in dashed lines for you to see. Make the vein first and then draw shallow, outward-facing Flower Petals (page 20) around the football shape. Make the end of the leaf point in the same direction as the end of the imaginary football, aligned with the inner vein.

THINK—in and back, outward points around the football

HOLLY TWIG

To make a Holly Twig, start by drawing Tight Cluster Berries (page 35). From between the berries, draw a Holly leaffacing outward. Notice that the top leaf uses the incoming vine from the berries as the center vein for that leaf. This is an option for most leaves, if you find it suits the area where your motif is placed. There is more on this subject in Making Leaves Travel (below).

MAKING LEAVES TRAVEL

Leaves won't do you any good if they don't have a branch. So, with every leaf, you need a vine. Once the leaf is finished, just backtrack down the center vein and beyond the leaf until you have room to shoot off with a new branch. Follow the new branch to the place where the next leaf needs to be.

THINK—in, back, leaf, down the stem, new branch; in, back, leaf, down the stem …

Fruit

Fruit and leaves go together very nicely. Here are some basics.

CHERRIES

Cherries are just a round loop at the end of a vine. Go to the end of the vine and make a 90° pivot to start the circle.

THINK—in, stop, around

For a cluster, when you finish the circle, retrace the stem to the top and repeat the Cherry as many times as you'd like.

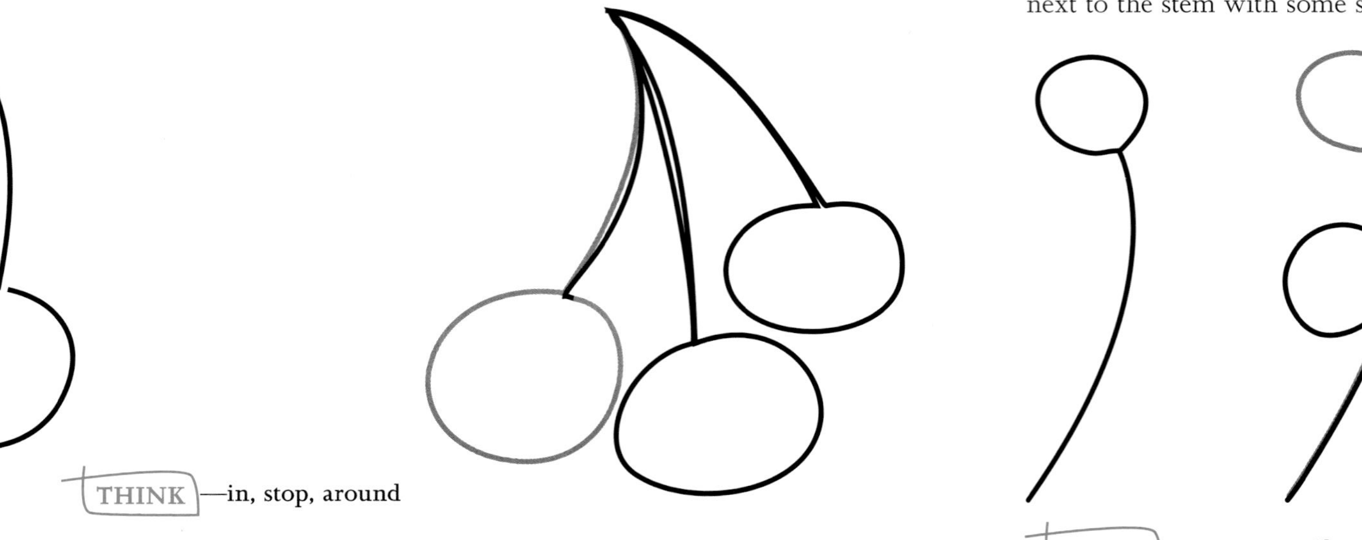

LOOSE CLUSTER BERRIES

Make a Loose Cluster of Berries by drawing a stem with a loop at the end that looks like a cherry. On the way back down the stem, place some round loops right next to the stem with some space between each loop.

THINK—curve to a Cherry, loops next to stem

TIGHT CLUSTER BERRIES

Berries in a tight cluster look a lot like clover. From the stem, turn and make a Cherry, and then draw more loops that start at the base of and share the walls of the original Cherry.

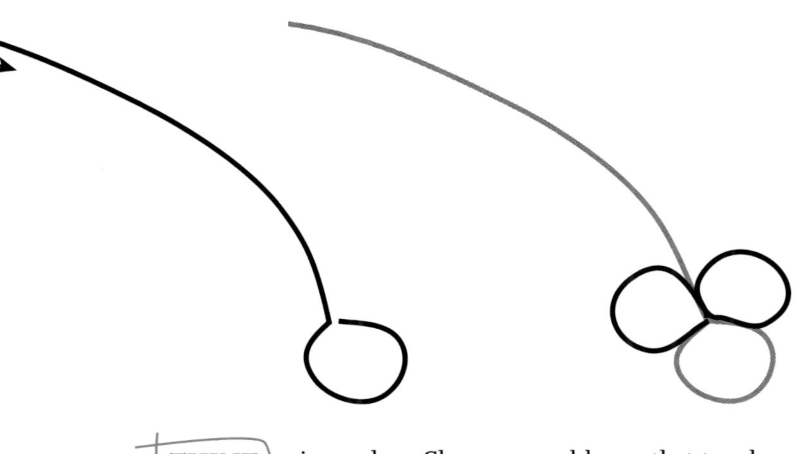

THINK—in, make a Cherry, round loops that touch

STRAWBERRIES

When you really look at them, you see that strawberries are very oddly shaped. They're sort of like an attempt at drawing a heart that failed in every aspect—not enough curve into the center, weak shoulders, and no point on the bottom. Sometimes the bottom is even tooth-shaped, like the Teeth design (page 19). Draw the stem to the top of the berry, make a weak shoulder to the left, curve in toward the rounded bottom, then go back up toward the top, curving gently outward for the shoulder, then back to the stem.

THINK—shoulder, in, around, out, shoulder

Add sepals to the berry by drawing 5 little leaves without veins that radiate from the stem's base.

Flowers with Centers

Like leaves, flowers are made to travel with a vine. Most flowers begin with a center. Those are most easily done by going into the center with the vine, making a 90° turn, and then drawing a circle of sorts before making the petals. It looks like a Cherry on a stem.

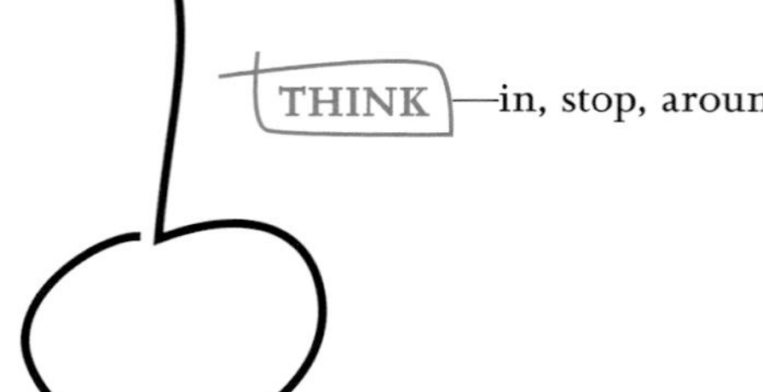

THINK—in, stop, around

DAISY

Daisies are made by adding flower petals—a row of simple arcs—around the center. Like leaves, Daisies must have a vine to connect them. The closer you can make the side of the first petal to the incoming vine, the less noticeable the vine will become.

THINK—in, around, follow the vine to petal, petal, petal … Follow the vine out.

SUNFLOWER

Sunflowers are just a large center surrounded by a row of short, fat Sunshines (page 20) and, outside of that, a row of big, tall Sunshines.

THINK—in, around, short Sunshines, tall Sunshines … Follow the vine out.

WILD ROSE

Wild Roses are similar to the Daisy (at left), with a single row of petals outside the center. But the center of a Wild Rose is more of an oval, so you can fit five or six Teeth-motif (page 19) petals around it.

THINK—in, oval, tooth, tooth … Follow the vine out.

CAMELLIA

Camellias are made like the Daisy (page 36) but with more rows of shorter petals. Each row of petals kisses the outer part of the petals in the row just to the center of it.

THINK—in, around, petals around the center, offset petals around again, offset petals around again, and follow the vine out

DAHLIA

These spiky Dahlias are made simply by drawing a small, round center with long Sunshines (page 20) around the outside.

THINK—in, around, long Sunshines … Follow the vine out.

DOUBLE DAHLIA

Go around the Dahlia again to make it double, or keep going around for a truly shaggy Dahlia!

THINK—in, around, long Sunshines, out a bit, long Sunshines … Follow the vine out.

FLOWER CENTER VARIATIONS

Any flower with a center can be changed by using a center variation.

Swirly Center

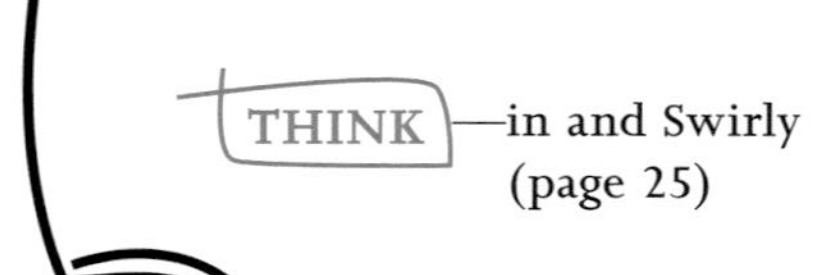

THINK—in and Swirly (page 25)

Meander Center

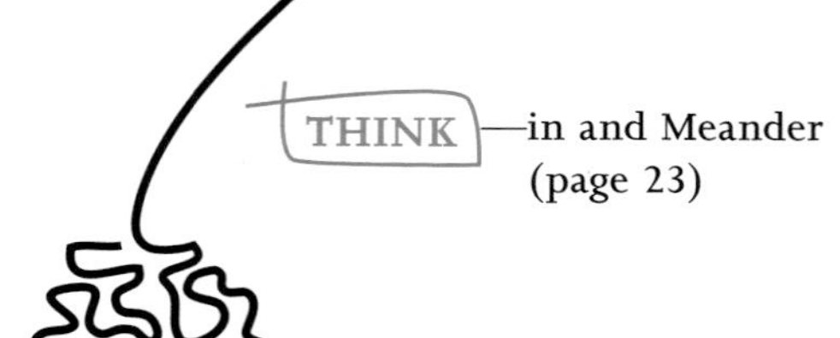

THINK—in and Meander (page 23)

Checkered Center

After finishing the center circle, make an arc that reaches the opposite side of the circle. Retrace up the circle a bit, echo back to the opposite side, retrace up the circle about the same amount as on the other side, and echo back. When you don't have room for any more, switch your arcs so they are perpendicular to the previous ones, and then repeat the arcing process.

THINK—arc, up, echo, up, echo … switch. Arc, over, echo, over, echo …

Outer Loops Center

THINK—in, around, Loops (page 11) around the outside of the center

Inner Circles Center

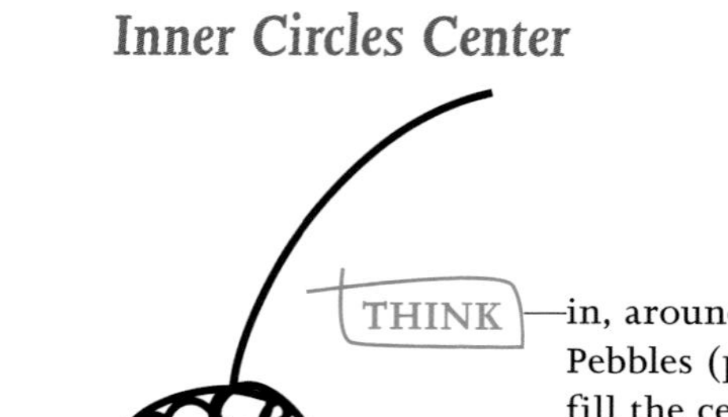

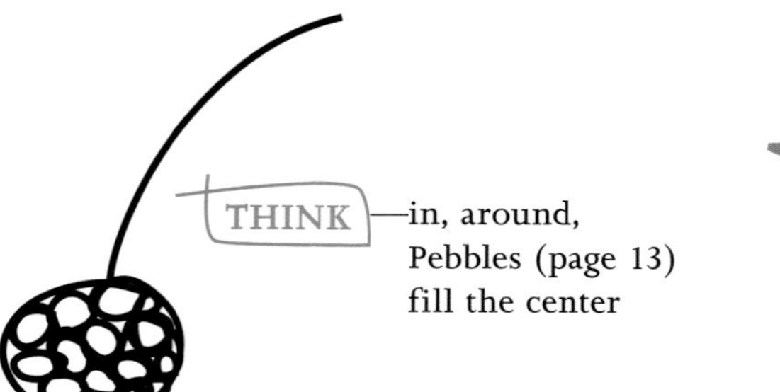

THINK—in, around, Pebbles (page 13) fill the center

Petal Flames

You can add texture to any flower with petals by adding Flames (page 16) around the center. This is best done after the petals have been made so the Flames can follow the petal contours. You can keep the Flames open at the base or keep them tight together.

Think about varying the size of the Flames and following the petal's contours.

Alternate Escape Route

Sometimes, because of where you are headed with your design, you need to get out of the flower center in a place different from where you came in. Just retrace around the center until you find the right place between petals to continue the vine.

THINK—around and around and "Let me out!"

Flowers without Centers

PLUMERIA

Plumeria is a simple five-petal flower made of Teardrops (page 45) that are joined along their lower sides. These are nice in bunches.

THINK—in, Teardrop, retrace, Teardrop, retrace, Teardrop … Follow the vine out.

GERANIUM

Geranium blossoms have five Teeth-shaped (page 19) petals that meet in the center with a curved vein into the middle of each petal.

THINK—in, Tooth and back to center, vein, and back … Follow the vine out.

IRIS

An Iris starts similar to a Geranium, but with only three downward-facing, veined, nearly Teeth-shaped petals (page 19). Instead of the dent on the top of the tooth going toward the center, bump it out a bit. Finish with two misshapen leaf petals for the top. Exit on the opposite side from where you began.

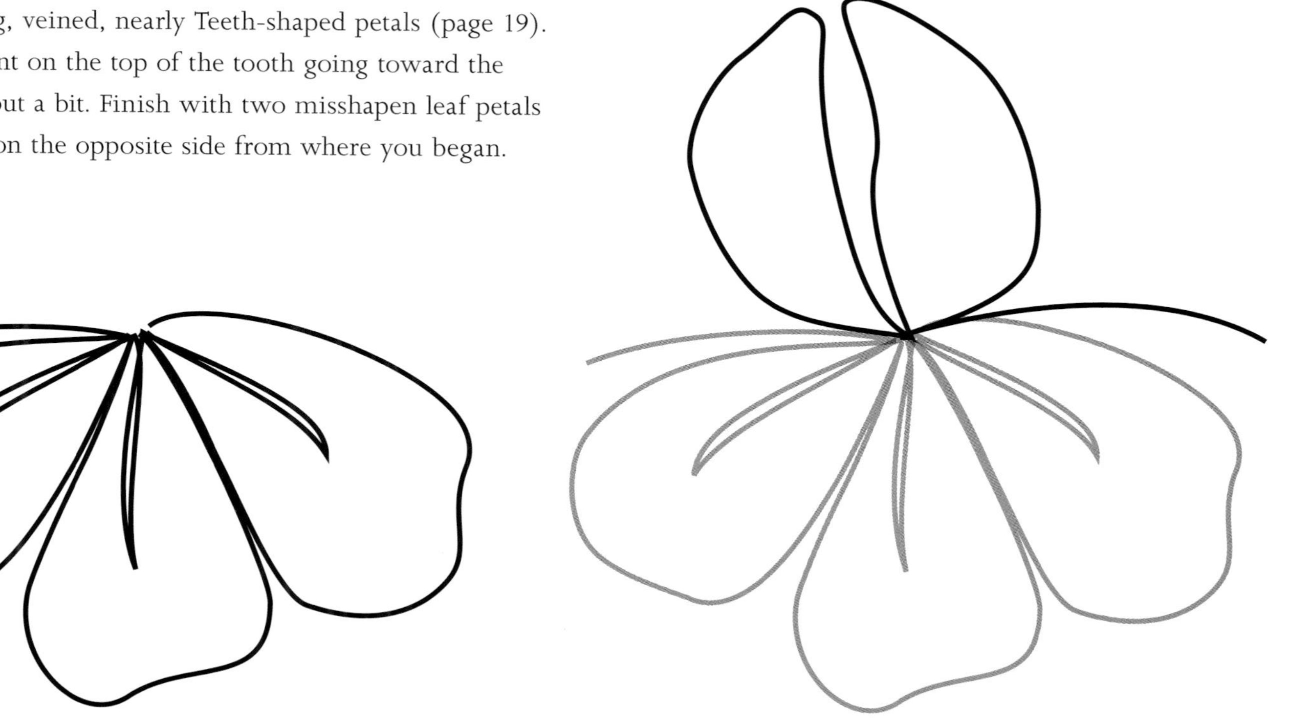

THINK—in, downward Tooth, and back to center; vein and back, times three; then upward leaf, upward leaf, and out

ROSE

It's easy to make beautiful roses. Start by coming in from one side and make a Hook (Question Mark) (page 24). Echo on the outside to the base of the Hook.

THINK—in, up, Hook, echo back down

Follow the incoming vine back out a bit, curve up, and kiss the Hook at its widest point. Continue on to make two Teeth (page 19), with the end of the second one kissing the Hook at the widest part of its left side. Turn from there and make a gentle arc down to the base of the Hook. This can be used by itself as a bud.

THINK—out and up, kiss the side, Tooth, Tooth, kiss, and turn, down

Trace back up the left side of the bud and make a Tooth that ends back at the base of the Hook. Follow the bottom of that petal out and around the bottom of the bud to make a huge Tooth petal that covers the whole bottom of the Rose. Come back to the base of the Hook along the vine where you came in.

THINK—trace up and out, Tooth and back, trace out and down, big long Tooth, and retrace back in

Retrace back out along the original vine a bit, go around the flower with rather shallow Tooth petals, kissing the inner petals at the end of each Tooth, until your Rose is full enough.

THINK—retrace out, up, and Tooth, kiss and Tooth, kiss and Tooth

A narrow echo nicely finishes off the Rose.

THINK—follow the path with consistent spacing

Other Doodles

BOOMERANG CIRCLES

Sometimes you need a row of circles that ends where it starts.

Make a row of rainbow arcs. THINK—consistent bumps

Complete the last circle and continue making inverted rainbow-shaped arcs, matching the first row until you're back where you started. Think about reflecting those consistent bumps and matching the points.

THE DOUBLE HOOK

This motif is used over and over. It's just a Question Mark (Hook) (page 24) with an outside echo back to its base.

THINK—Hook up and follow it back

HEARTS

Hearts are just two reflecting Question Marks (page 24). Resist the temptation to expect perfection—you're not in grade school anymore! You can begin from the top, as in a leaf, or from the bottom.

THINK—Question Mark and Question Mark

STARS

Just like in first grade, you can finish off the final arm of the star by crossing over the original line or by kissing the original line and changing direction, depending on your space availability.

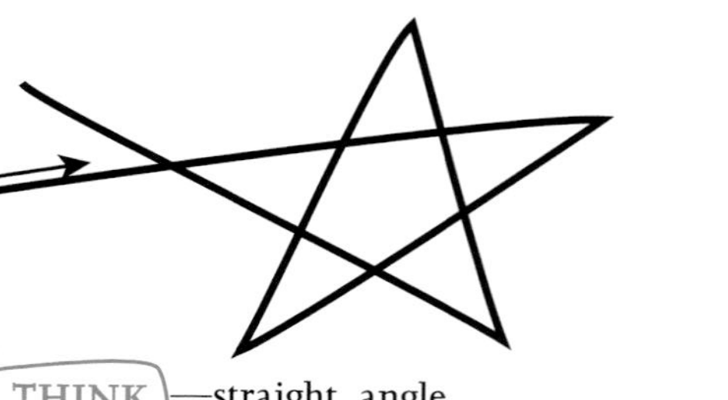

THINK—straight, angle, straight, angle …

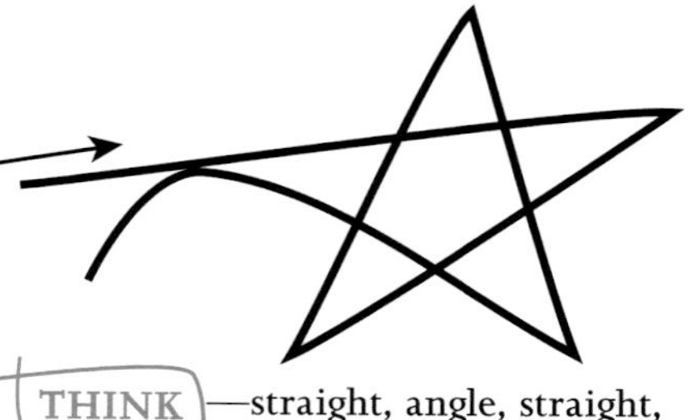

THINK—straight, angle, straight, angle … kiss and turn

SINGLE TEARDROPS

This Teardrop is a closed flower petal.

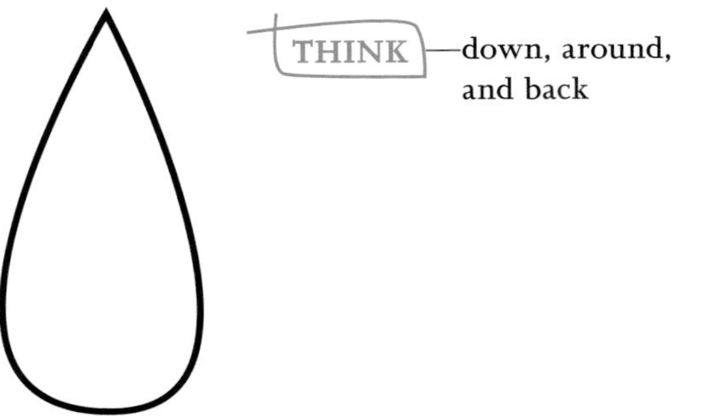

THINK—**down, around, and back**

RIBBONS

Ribbons are a useful motif for any quilt in which you are incorporating some kind of vine design. Because they are a Boomerang (you start and end at the same point) and they can fill a long, skinny space, you may find yourself partway through a quilt and need to use one to fill an awkward space. Just be sure to repeat it somewhere, so it looks like you did it on purpose!

THINK—**curve out, slanted end, exaggerate the curve back**

CHRISTMAS TREE

Although this motif doesn't exactly stop where it starts, it serves as a stand-alone design and can be used in the same way as most other Boomerangs. Start by making three sides of a box for the trunk. Then make small L's on alternating sides that get continuously smaller as the tree gets taller. Top it with a star, of course! Or you can start at the star and work down if that fits your space better.

THINK—**box, large-to-small L's, star on top**

feathers

feath•er (noun) [fĕth´ ər]—plumage consisting of numerous slender, closely arranged parallel teardrops on either side of a tapering, partly hollow vein

Every quilter wants to be able to make feathers, but most of us think they are beyond our skill level—and even beyond anything we could ever achieve. That's just not so! You may not be able to jump right into fancy Victorian feathers, but if you can doodle a smooth line, a teardrop, and a question mark, you can make a feather of some sort. Practicing feather doodles will help you make big improvements. Be sure to practice feathers going up, down, to the right, and to the left, so you can use them anywhere.

Single-Stem Proper Feathers

Proper Feathers keep their sides touching, so that with every Hook (page 24), you must trace along the side of the previous hook. Still, it is only a series of Hooks or Question Marks on a stem.

Note If you do not wish to make the Hooks from the bottom up, you can retrace the stem as the first step on the feather's second side. In this scenario, the second side is made as an exact reflection of the first side. Careful! The center stem can get a bit thread-heavy if you are not precise.

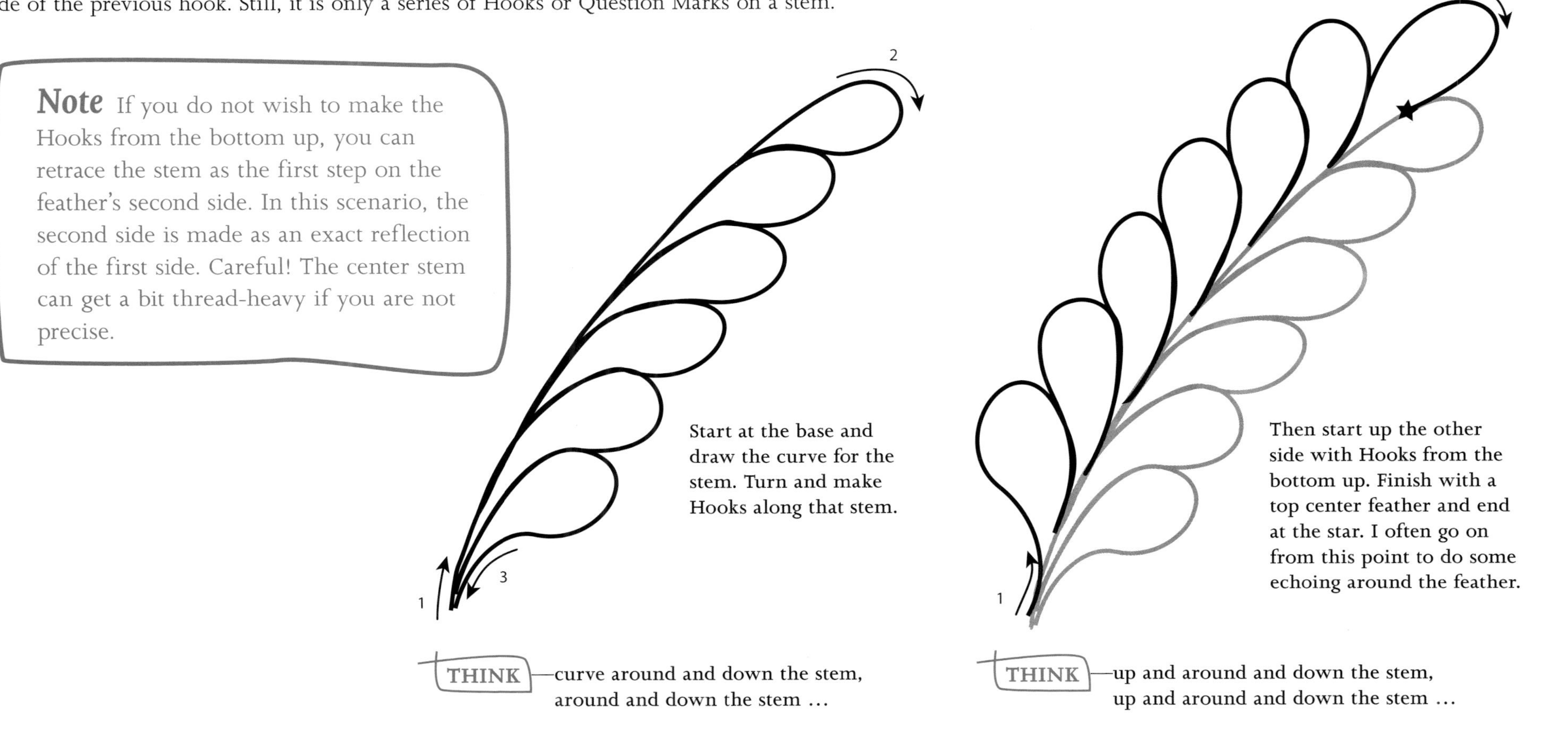

Start at the base and draw the curve for the stem. Turn and make Hooks along that stem.

THINK—curve around and down the stem, around and down the stem …

Then start up the other side with Hooks from the bottom up. Finish with a top center feather and end at the star. I often go on from this point to do some echoing around the feather.

THINK—up and around and down the stem, up and around and down the stem …

Victorian Feathers

These are the most elegant feathers of all—and they are actually much easier than they look. The sequence is significantly different for making these feathers. Each feather looks like it's partially hidden behind the one below it.

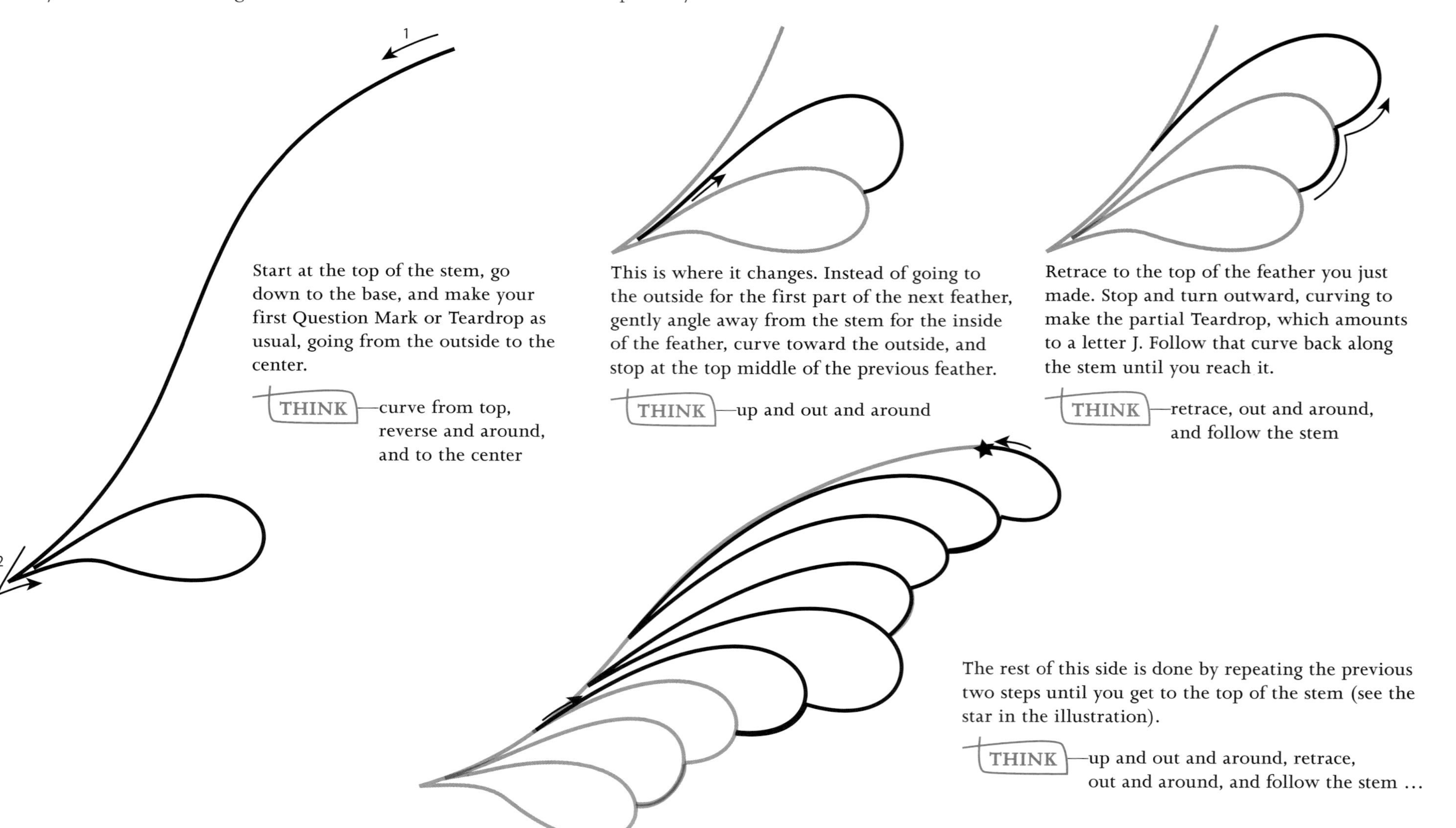

Start at the top of the stem, go down to the base, and make your first Question Mark or Teardrop as usual, going from the outside to the center.

THINK—curve from top, reverse and around, and to the center

This is where it changes. Instead of going to the outside for the first part of the next feather, gently angle away from the stem for the inside of the feather, curve toward the outside, and stop at the top middle of the previous feather.

THINK—up and out and around

Retrace to the top of the feather you just made. Stop and turn outward, curving to make the partial Teardrop, which amounts to a letter J. Follow that curve back along the stem until you reach it.

THINK—retrace, out and around, and follow the stem

The rest of this side is done by repeating the previous two steps until you get to the top of the stem (see the star in the illustration).

THINK—up and out and around, retrace, out and around, and follow the stem …

From the star, repeat the steps from the beginning as a reflection, making the second stem with feathers starting from the bottom. The stem can be traced, echoed, or a different curve altogether. The one shown here is a loose echo. These feathers are especially suited to fill odd spaces because all the feathers don't have to be the same size. The upper portion of this one nicely fills this page. When the feathers start to get too long for you to keep a smooth line, start a shorter series of feathers—like I did in the middle of the second side. When you reach the top feather of the first side, finish off your last few feathers, and end at the dot.

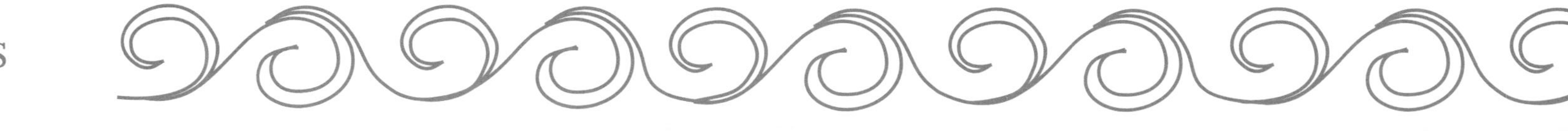

Embellishments

INSIDE THE FEATHER

Here are a few ideas for embellishing the inside of any feather. The extras in the first and the third examples can be incorporated as you make the feather, or you can add any of the embellishments later.

Veins on the left, pointed leaves on the right

Add a circle on the ends of the feathers as you go by making an extra loop when you reach the top of each feather. Multiple circles can be added after the individual feather is finished. This is most effective when you select to embellish only a few feathers. Boomerang Circles (page 44) work the best, so that you can get back to the stem without having to retrace the side of the feather. Multiple Boomerang Circles (page 44) are shown on the left and single Loop circles (page 11) on the right.

Adding a Teardrop in the center of each feather is a nice touch when you need a little something extra. Here, a Teardrop is tucked in neatly on the left and a larger one is used on the right.

OUTSIDE THE FEATHER

I love the look of a dot at the top of each feather.

Just echo close to the outside of the motif and place a round loop at the top of each feather.

THINK—echo and loop, echo and loop …

Putting a little bit of Sunshine (page 20) on the top of each feather gives the feathers a more organic look. Echo to a point at the top of each feather and down to a point between them.

THINK—up to a point, down to a point …

Adding another echo outside of that dot makes it look like eyelet lace. Think about keeping consistent spacing.

Echoing closely several times around feathers helps to separate them from their surroundings. Think about keeping consistent spacing.

Ferns

In my world, these are called Fernies. Whatever you call them, they are similar to Feathers (page 46) in structure, but with different kinds of plumage.

ROUND FERNY

A Round Ferny consists of a stem that starts at the base with Excited Water (page 22) for plumage. Notice that I have left a loose line after the last ripple at the top. From there, you can either travel to another motif or retrace the stem back down to the base.

THINK—curve up the stem, Excited Water down, turn at the base, Excited Water up, turn the last ripple at the top parallel to the stem

FOREST FERNY

This is a stem with Sunshines (page 20) for fronds.

THINK—curve up the stem, Sunshines down, turn, Sunshines up, top it off

Draw the stem starting at the base, then go back down with Sunshines that get longer as you go down. When you reach the base of the stem, turn and make more Sunshines on the way back up, getting shorter as you go up. Finish it off with a face-up Sunshine. From there, you can either go on to the next motif or go back down the stem.

BABY FOREST FERNY

For this baby version of the Forest Ferny (at left), start with an extra curvy stem and come back down on the inside of the curve with Teeth (page 19).

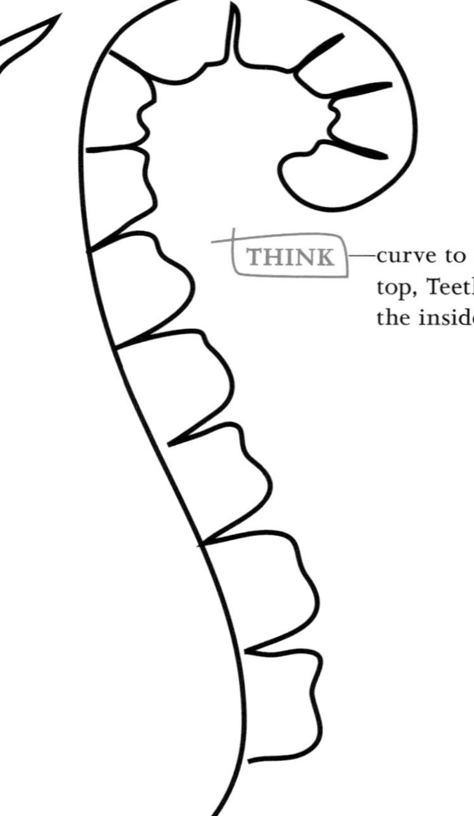

THINK—curve to the top, Teeth down the inside

JUVENILE FOREST FERNY

This is a combination of the previous two Fernies.

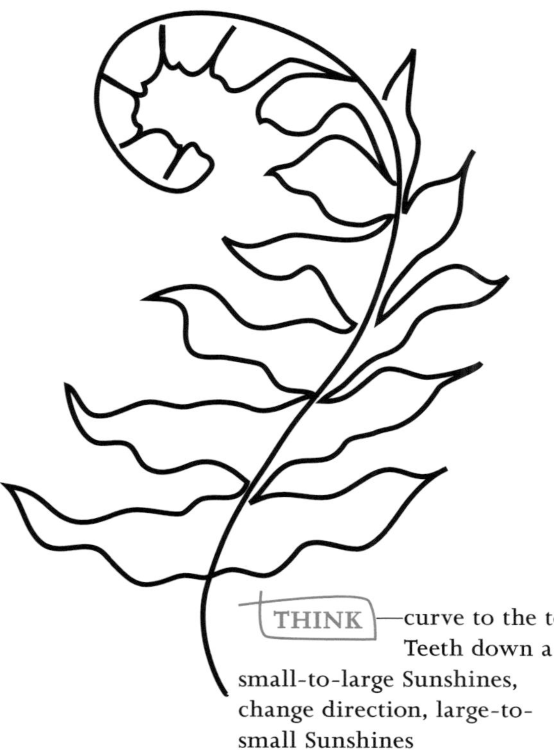

THINK—curve to the top, Teeth down a bit, small-to-large Sunshines, change direction, large-to-small Sunshines

Start at the base and draw an extra-curvy stem. Start from the top of the stem with Teeth (page 19) on the inside of the curve and then move to ever-larger Sunshines (page 20) to the base of the stem. Repeat the Sunshines on the opposite side of the stem, getting smaller and stopping when you get to the Teeth on the other side. From there you can go back down the stem or move on.

PALM FERNY

Maybe this isn't really a Ferny, but it's kind of a frond. It is made like the Braided Feather (page 47).

THINK—out left to a point, back to the center, out right to a point, back to the center … up to a point and back to the center

Start at the base and draw the outside of each leaf, then go to the center every time, alternating sides. There is no central stem—instead, you finish each leaf by kissing the inside of the last leaf you made. Finish it off with a leaf that points upward.

CELEBRATION FERNY

This Ferny is made like a Double-Stem Finger Feather (page 48), only after you make the stem, you can throw in all kinds of things for the plumage, including finger feathers, Leaves (page 31), Double Hooks (page 24), and Ribbons (page 45). So much fun!

THINK—up, and "Hmmm, what can I add next?" Repeat for the other side.

ensembles

en•sem•ble (noun) [ŏn sŏm´bəl]—a unit or group of complementary parts that contribute to a single effect

"All those motifs are good and fine," you say. "But what do I do with these great designs?" I've put together some of my favorite ensembles for you to practice. While you're tracing, watch where each motif takes you, so you can repeat it on your own. Have fun!

Anatomy of an Ensemble

There are reasons these ensembles work. I make a set of rules for each quilt before I ever take a quilting stitch. These rules give me the freedom to quilt without the stress of thinking I may end up somewhere I don't want to be and not be able to get back.

THE RULES

1. Decide ahead of time how far apart your quilting is going to be spaced. Try to keep the shapes consistent, but don't concern yourself with making them exactly the same.

2. Choose the motifs and practice them before you start.

3. Always include at least one Traveler. Use it to go to another place on the quilt or to get through tight spaces.

4. Start in an inconspicuous place. For a domestic-machine quilter, that place will probably be along a seam in the quilt's center. For a longarm quilter, it will probably be off the edge of the quilt.

5. Elongate a shape to fill the space to the edge when there's not room to add something else in that place.

6. Shorten a shape to make the motif fit in a desired space.

7. When using Finger Feathers (page 48), if there isn't room to make another feather because making that next feather would not leave enough room to turn around, allow yourself to make that shape backward. It fills the space available without being too tight, and it puts you in the perfect place to begin the next motif.

8. Keep the motifs or motif sets close together and evenly spaced by filling in all of an area before leaving it.

9. Add Ribbons (page 45) to backfill odd shapes.

In the illustration at right, I have noted where I employed different rules. The numbers in the illustrations correspond to the rules.

Let's look more closely at the illustration. On the left side and along the top, you will see several references to Rule 5. If you start tracing from the beginning, you see the first one is on the last feather around the first Teardrop 1-2-3 (page 28). I knew I needed to echo back from there, but there wasn't room for anything else, so I just made that feather longer. Trace around the rest of the illustration and see that is the case every time there are longer-than-usual feathers. When I'm up against boundaries, the available space dictates the length of the feathers. The same holds true in the three instances of Rule 6, where the feathers are shorter than they would be if I had been in open space.

Find the reference to Rule 7 near the center of the illustration. Right before I got to that reference, I was moving up toward the set of feathers above the 7. You can see that if I had put in another whole feather, there wouldn't have been room to turn around. By going to the far side of this last feather and curving back toward the previous feather, it brought me back around to where I needed to be to begin the echoing. The little almost-feather, almost-teardrop that formed is a common shape in this ensemble and will not stick out as a mistake or oddity.

Find the three references to Rule 3. One of them comes right after the Rule 7 reference just discussed. I was in the upper middle section of my drawing, but had left an area below and to the left with nothing in it. So I used the echo to get back down to where I could point some feathers toward the left part of the design. After that set of motifs and the one following, I was nearly at the bottom of the area, with no room for anymore motifs. So, I employed Rule 3 again to echo around to a better place for the next set of motifs. Note that I did not echo the shape I had just drawn; rather, I echoed one that was laid down before. Take advantage of the rules you set and use them whenever it suits you. The last reference to Rule 3 on the right side of the illustration also is used on a shape that was not the most recent shape to be drawn.

Look at the illustration on the next page to see the route I took around the area (Rule 8). My goal was to finish everything in one area before going onto the next, covering the whole section with evenly spaced motifs. My route is not the end-all-be-all; it's just an example of how I managed to cover the entire area. You could be more methodical and just go up and down, but varying the way you work across an area will help give your quilt a custom-quilted look rather than the look of a pantograph (which, by the way, I have no problem with; I just can't follow them).

Notice how, with nearly every curve in the path of the motifs, I worked to keep the motifs right next to each other and fill the outer edges of the space. In a whole quilt, there wouldn't be as much emphasis on the outer edge all the time, but it is always helpful to be aware of your space limitations.

Quilting in this way has a certain rhythm. When you finish a Teardrop 1-2-3, you already know the next thing you'll do is surround it with Finger Feathers. Then you know you're going to echo to the place where you want to start the next set of motifs. You don't waste time thinking up what to do next because you've already decided. The stitching itself becomes relaxing and stress free.

Take a look at the Forest Fernies + Loops + Wild Roses + Simple Leaves ensemble on page 74. How many of the rules can you find? The Forest Fernies themselves are shaped differently, even though they are all recognizable as the same motif. Ribbons fill odd spaces, illustrating Rule 9. Now use an analytical eye to check out the other ensembles in this chapter. The rules I chose for each ensemble are obvious once you know what they are.

The following are just a few of the many ensembles you could use to cover a quilt. Try mixing different motifs together. My hope is that you will use this section as a resource to build on in your quilting journey. Experiment and make this an adventure!

Loops + Simple Leaves + Daisies

Vines + Echoing + Swirlies

For this, you start with a vine—a simple curved line. Stop and double back with an echo, but exaggerate every curve by making the "hills" farther apart and the "valleys" closer together.

When you end up with a space that is too small to continue echoing into, fill that space with a Swirly (page 25). After the Swirly, the vine takes off in a new direction.

After the star, which is the end of the previous two steps, continue to fill the area by making the hills higher and the valleys lower. Notice the dot at the bottom right side of the page. At that point, you begin to double back on the opposite side of the original line that began with the star. To keep things interesting, every place that was treated like a hill on the other side of this line is treated like a valley on this side, and every valley like a hill. So one side of the original curve has echoes farther apart, while on the opposite side they are closer together. If you use this principle when you are making this ensemble on your own, it promises to be interesting!

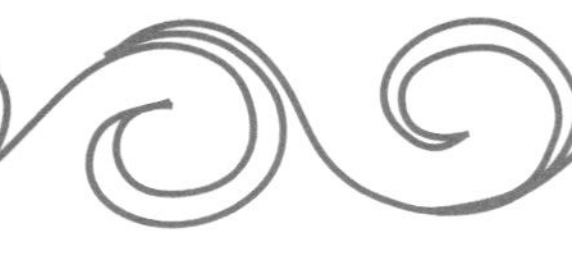

Teardrop 1-2-3's + Flower Petals + Echoing

Very cheery!

Swirlies + Finger Feathers + Echoing

One of my go-to ensembles!

Double-Stem Finger Feathers + Echoing

Double Hooks + Finger Feathers + Flames + Echoing

The focus here is on filling the space rather than making perfectly formed plumes. I kept the points a little offset from the stems, so it will be easier to trace.

This puts a little space between the Finger Feathers (page 48).

Meandering + Echoing

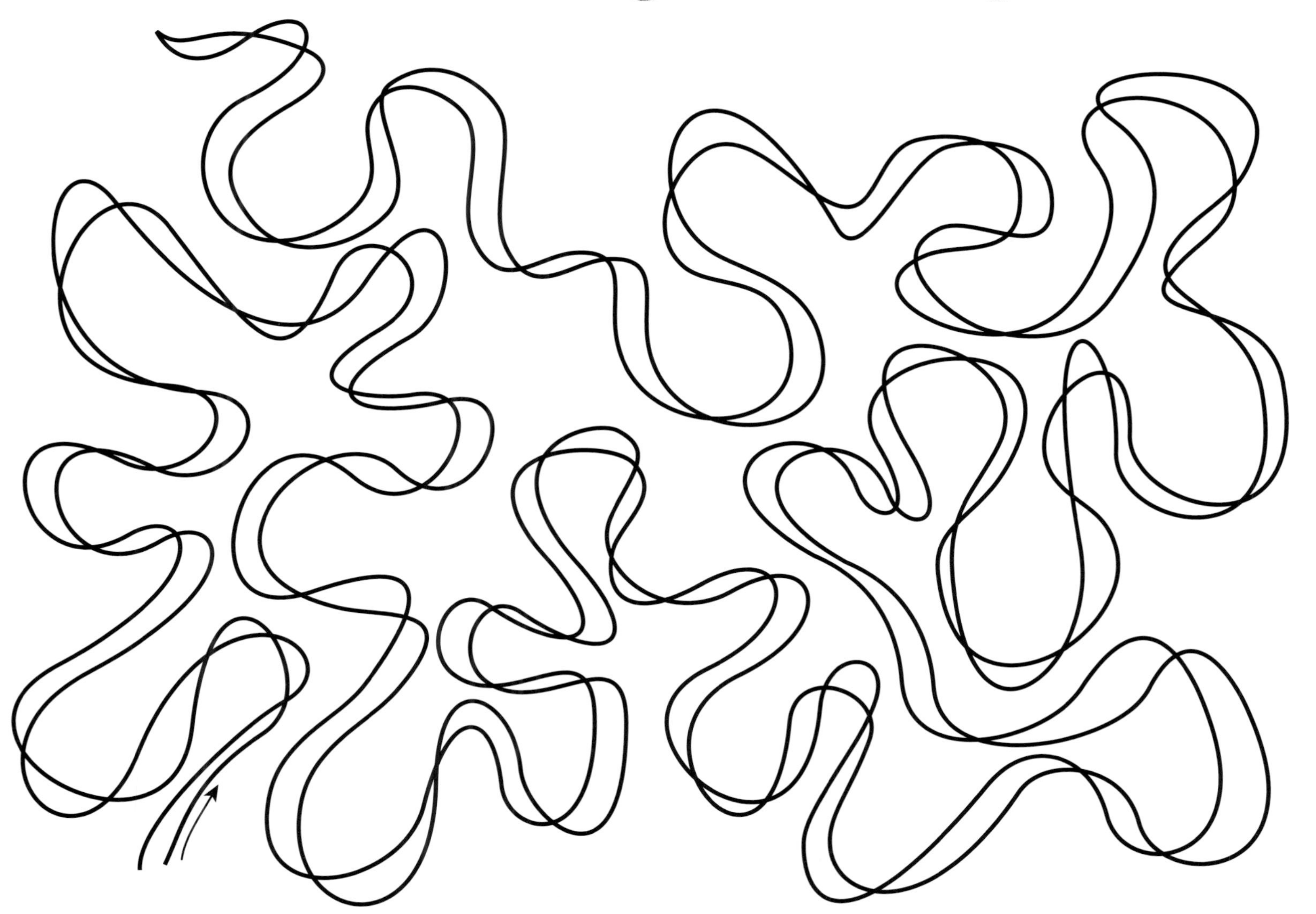

This is so much more interesting than simple, large Meandering (page 23)! Meander across an area and double back with an echo, exaggerating every curve and crossing the path frequently.

Irises + Flames

An instant field of irises!

Oak Leaf + Ivy Leaf + Loops + Ribbons

Perfect for a fall-themed quilt!

Excited Water + Echoing +Loops + Flower Petals

This is a fun and easy Ensemble. The first batch of Excited Water (page 22) motifs rotate around an imaginary circle, so they look like a 1960s flower-power motif or a splat of paint. If you need to get to a different place to start a new set, repeat a row of Echoing or Excited Water.

Roses + Loops + Half Simple Leaf + Echoing

While you're tracing, notice how well the echoing helps finish off the leaves around the Roses.

Rose with Meander Center + Simple Leaf + Ribbon + Plumeria + Vines

This makes a beautiful all-over design that draws the viewer into the quilt.

Teardrop 1-2-3's + Finger Feathers + Echoing

I love this design and use it all the time.

Forest Fernies + Loops + Wild Roses + Simple Leaves

Fresh from where the wild things grow!

Dividing the Space

Sometimes it's fun to just divide up the space with some long, curving vines with echoes and then fill each space with something different. This will probably involve starting and stopping, so it will take longer, but the results can be spectacular!

making it fit

Fit (verb, adj.) [fĭt]—to cause to be the proper size and shape; adapted to an end, a design, or an environment

Although my favorite quilting involves allover designs, there are times when it is helpful to know how to get in and out of shapes. Here are some thoughts on that, as well as some ideas for using some of the motifs presented earlier in more specific ways.

Getting In and Out of Points with Travelers

Sometimes you will want to fill one part of a block and not another, for a popping effect. In the illustration below, the first block shows the basic path to take with your motif.

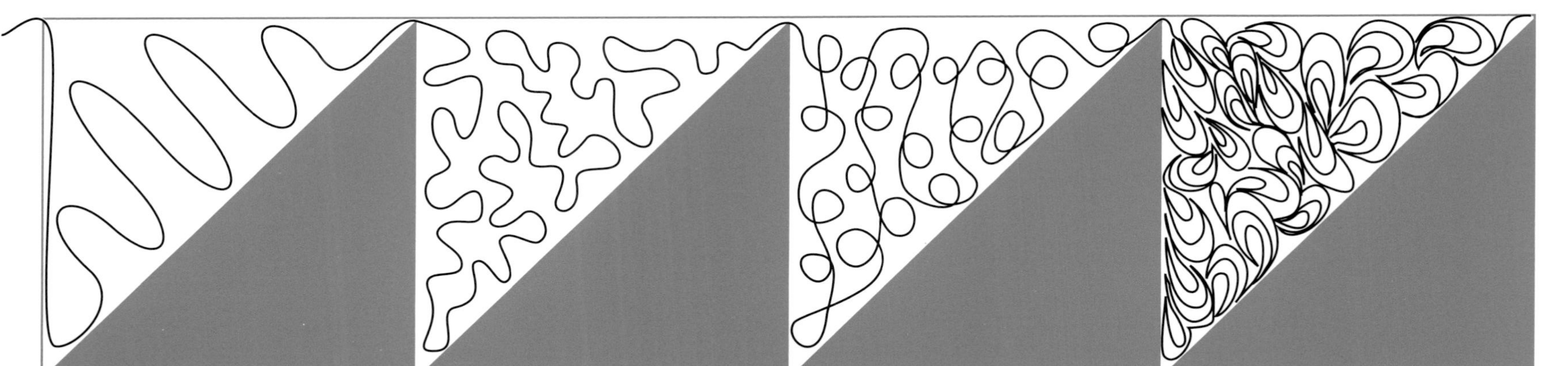

Start by hugging the closest seam and go all the way to the farthest point. Then go back and forth, filling the remaining area until you get to the edge of the block, where you'll cross over into the next one. The path is similar no matter which Traveler you choose.

Excited Water in Triangles

When you want to fill half a row of half-square triangles with Excited Water (page 22), just adjust the length of each wave to fit the area in the triangle and squirt out at the narrow point to begin the next triangle.

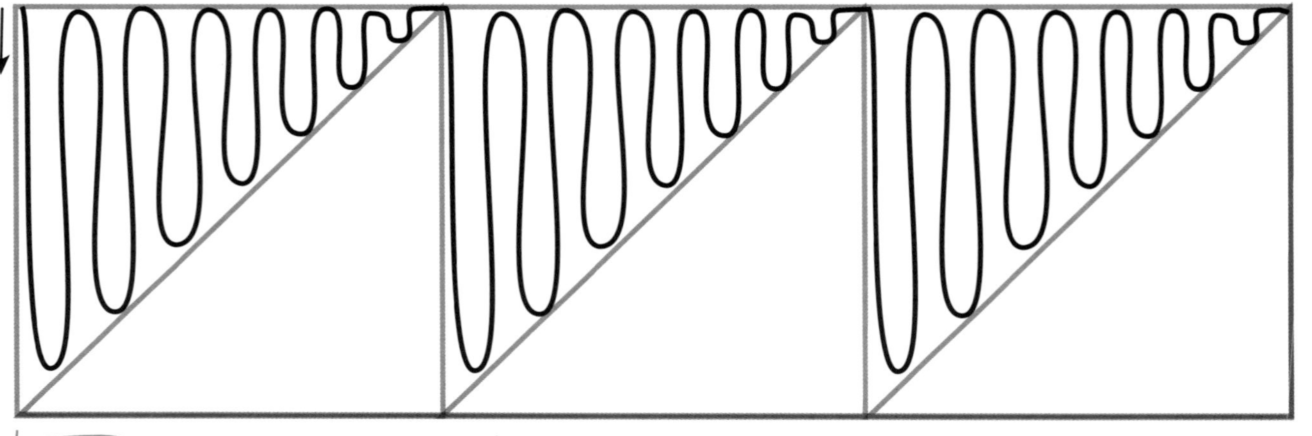

THINK—up and down and up and down … Follow the shape. Up and down and up and down …

You also can fill in all the triangles by making the waves in the second triangle perpendicular to the waves in the first triangle. Start on the right with the waves going side to side. When you get to the narrowest part, enter the triangle to the left that forms the rest of that block. Everything in that triangle will go up and down. The only trick is to have your last stroke in that triangle be a downward stroke so you can begin the next side-to-side waves in the third triangle.

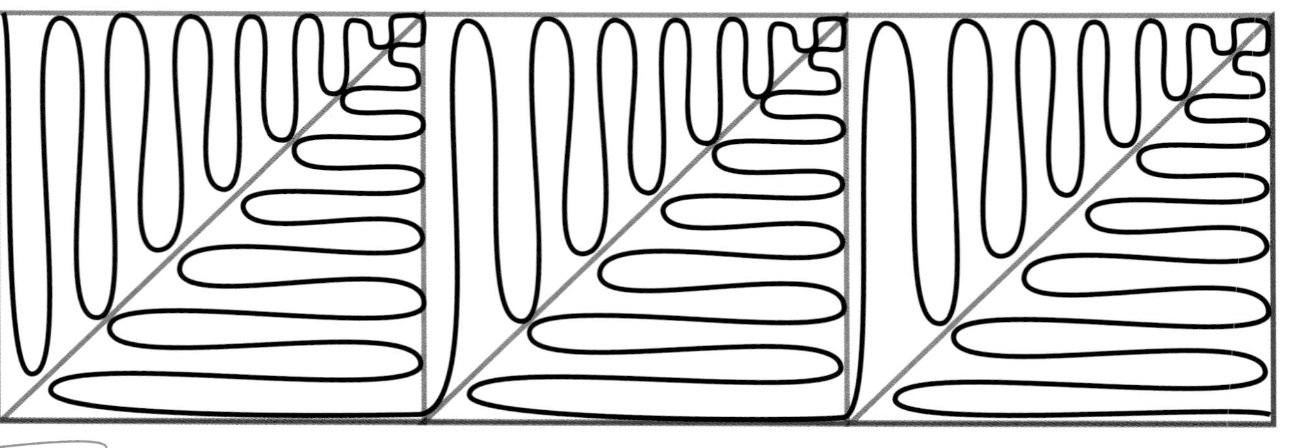

THINK—side to side … then up and down, ending on down … then side to side

Recently I've quilted lots of quilts with Stars comprised of diamond shapes. Making a sort of "Scroll Tree" is very useful for filling those diamonds. Starting at the center of the diamond, I alternate the direction of each scroll as I go upward, and I branch out as needed to fill in the sides symmetrically. When I get to the top, I just follow the long side of each Scroll down to the base and begin the next big diamond.

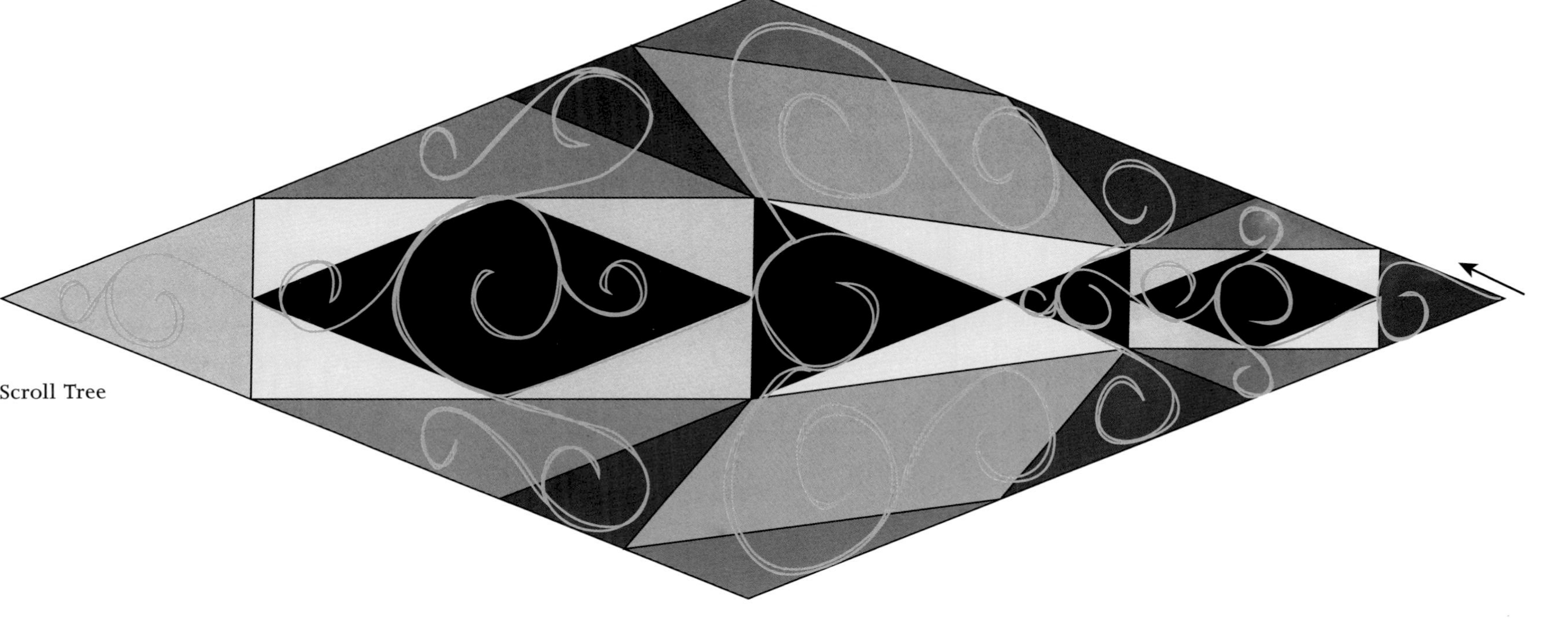

Scroll Tree

Oh, Those L's and E's!

When I was doing longarm quilting for hire, I would often challenge myself to quilt a whole quilt using just one set of motifs in different ways. One of those was cursive lowercase L's and E's. Here are some of those designs.

L'S AND E'S IN A NINE-PATCH

This particular design does require starting and stopping. I marked the start and stop places here with a dot. The L's are placed at the center of each light block and in the corners of all the dark patches. The E's are placed so the top of each is on the seam between the patches.

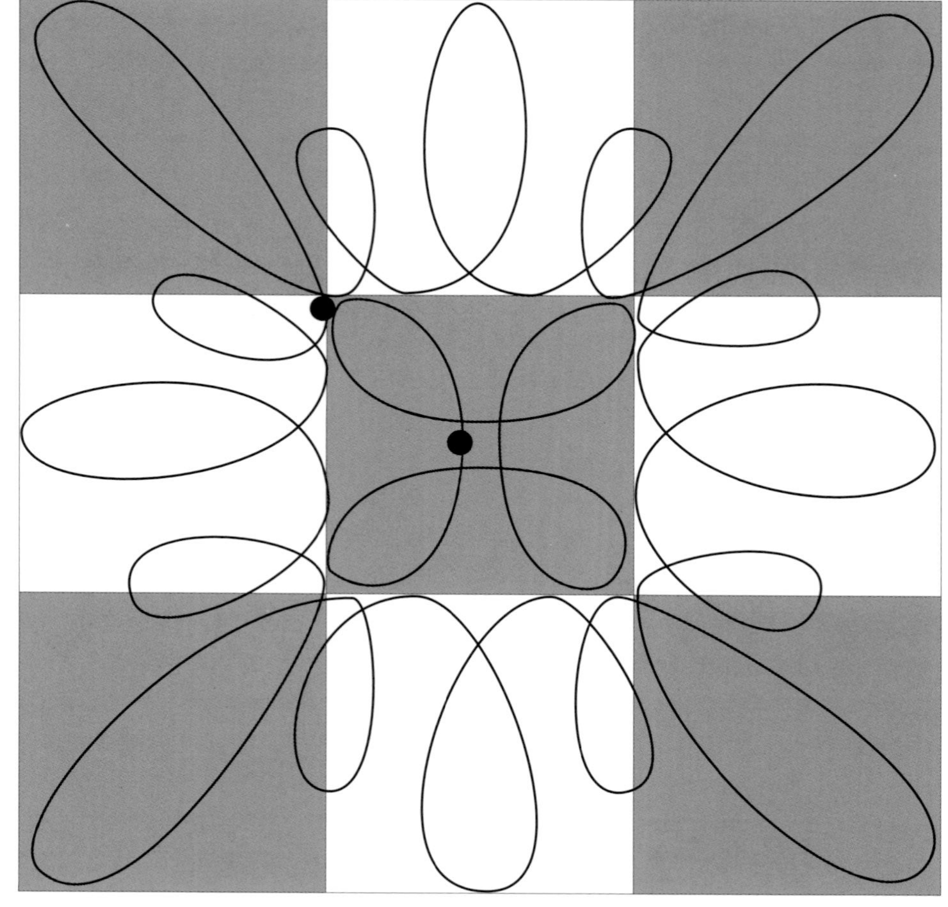

L'S AND E'S IN FLYING GEESE

This is easy. Just use the height of the triangle to determine the height of the L or E.

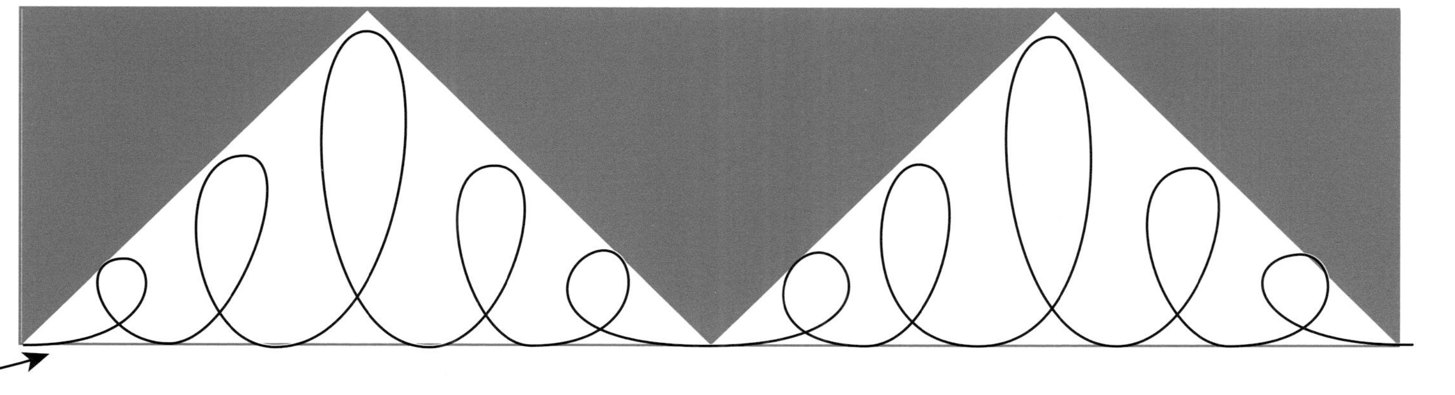

L'S AND E'S IN A BORDER

Start this one by using a temporary marker to draw the curve in the middle. Or you could keep it straight. If you have small blocks along the border, use them to keep your spacing consistent by putting all your L's at a seam and all the E's in between. Travel along the entire length of the border and then go back on the other side of the curve.

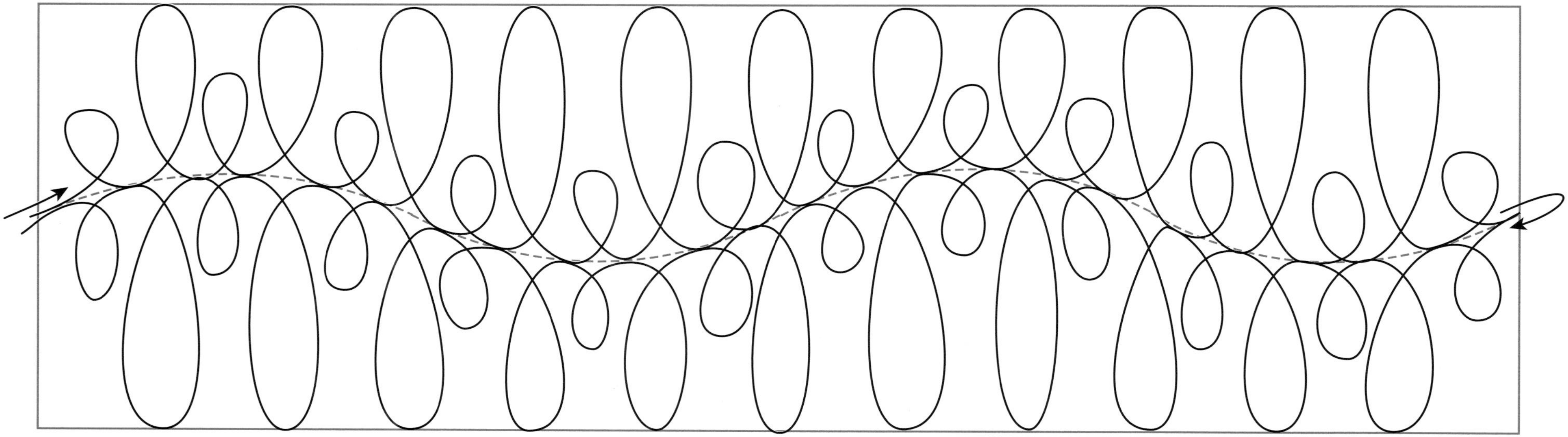

ALTERNATING L'S IN A BORDER

If your border is not surrounded by small blocks, it is useful to temporarily mark intervals to keep the L's evenly spaced. Just aim to make the top of each L touch that mark. The thing to remember when drawing this design is that you're always going to the far side of the loop first, just like when you are writing in cursive.

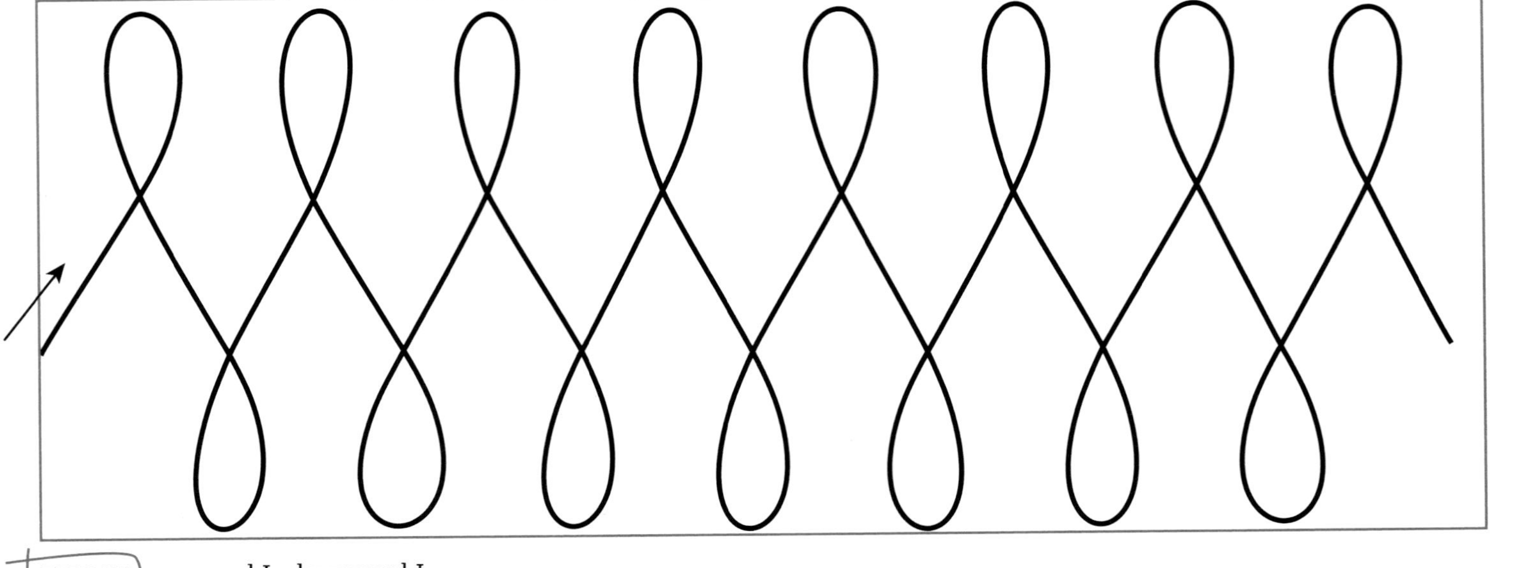

THINK—upward L, downward L

If you double back on the original design, repeating the same thing between the existing motifs, it makes an even more interesting border.

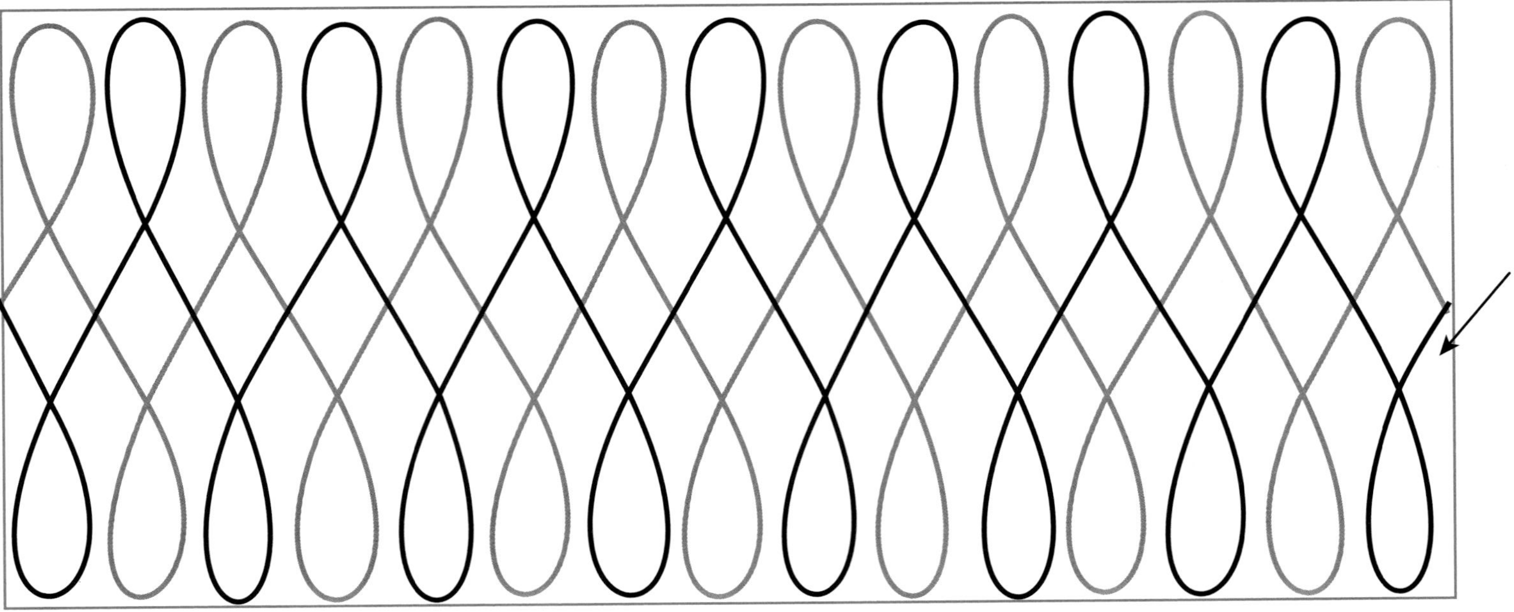

Fitting Feathers

When you want feathers in a specific shape, employ the rules—especially Rules 3, 5, and 6 (page 59)—and treat the block or shape like a whole quilt.

Employ Rules 5 and 6 (page 59) to fit a feather into a triangle or to turn a corner by curving the stem and filling the space.

Start in the center and use the Double-Stem Proper Feathers (page 49) with Traveling Circles as a Stem Filler (page 50) and an echo around one side to take you back to the center, where you start again. The sequence is right side stem to the block corner, feathers down the right side, left side stem, and feathers back down, Traveling Circles (page 13) from the center to the end of the stem, then echo back to the beginning. Then you start on the next square.

Grid Work

Grid work is filling a specific shape—whether a square, diamond, or triangle—by repeating a specific motif. The grid can be made up of patches of a certain shape or drawn onto the quilt top in open space with a temporary marker.

EXCITED WATER GRID WORK

The thing to figure out here is how many waves you can consistently draw and still get to the next gridded area in the correct position. If you can keep it looking consistent, the actual number of lines is not important. Note that mine are not all exactly the same.

THINK—up and down and up and down, back and forth and back and forth …

CALM WATER GRID WORK

Most people call this design continuous curve or orange peel. But since we've already established this shape as Calm Water, I'm sticking to it! This form of grid work is suited to rectangles, diamonds, and triangles. The junctions can be either patch corners or a temporary grid. There is a way to do this that will not leave you with unfinished areas—I, however, tend to wander off and then end up going back to finish something. Maybe next time I'll look at my own directions. Maybe.

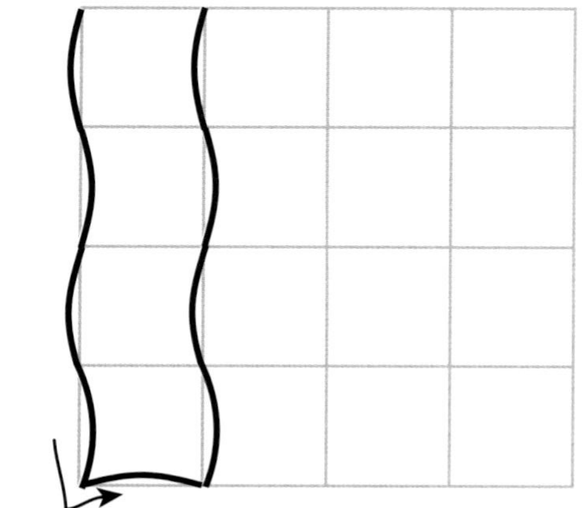

1. Start down an edge and make gentle waves on alternating sides of the seamline, crossing over at each patch corner. Go all the way to the far end and over one patch. Then go all the way up again. Think about keeping the distance from the height of the curve to the seam consistent and crossing directly over the seam.

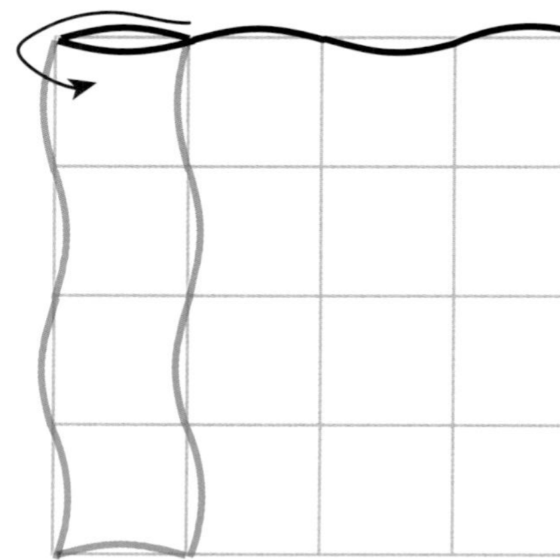

2. From the top of the second row, head back toward the first line, kiss that corner, and reflect that curve back to the second row, making a football. Then follow that line to the farthest horizontal point to the right.

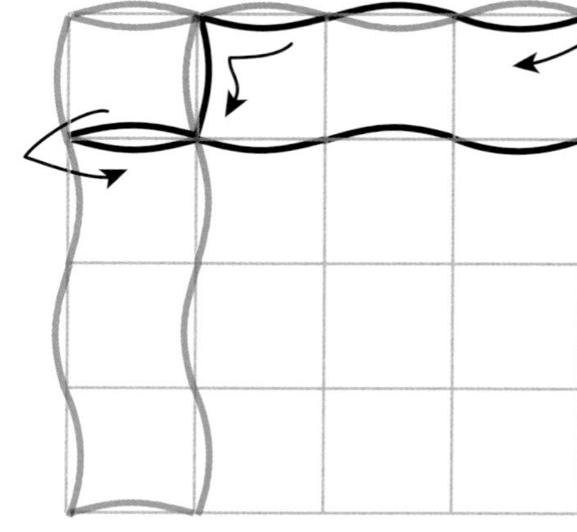

3. Make a U-turn and curve your way back to the second vertical row, reflecting each curve on the opposite side of the seamline. Turn downward for one patch. Then repeat Step 2.

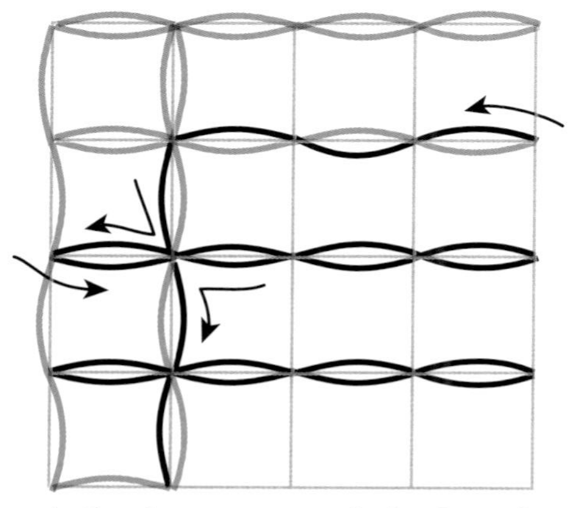

4. Continue to repeat the horizontal rows, going down one patch upon returning to that second vertical row.

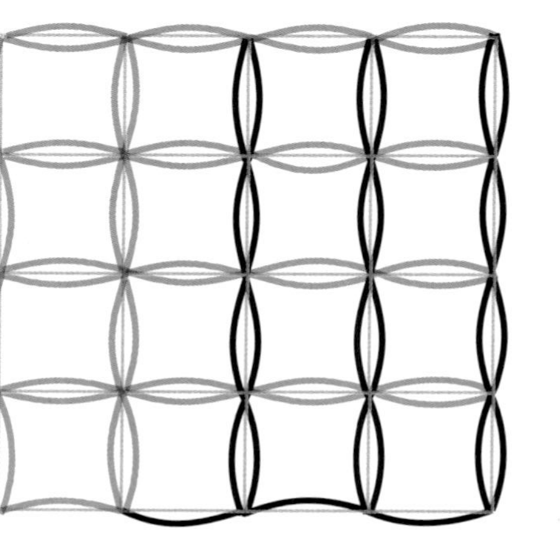

5. Curve toward the right and the next row. Stop and curve back and forth up to the top, and then turn and come back down as you did for the horizontal rows.

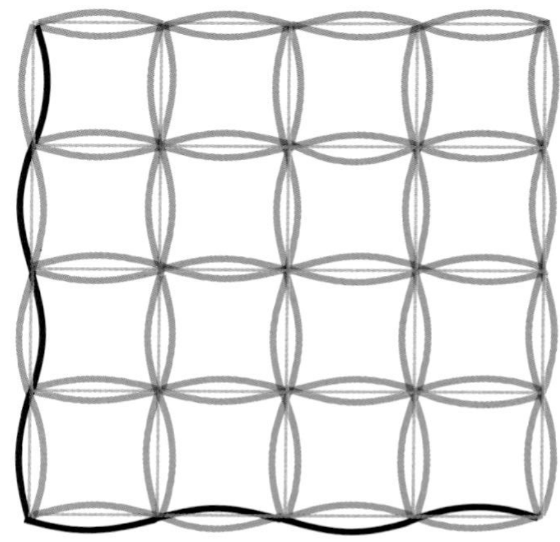

6. Finish it off by reflecting the curves around the outside edge and back to the starting point.

about the AUTHOR

Photo by Terry Day

Cheryl Malkowski lives in Roseburg, Oregon, with her husband, Tom. She has two grown children and two grandchildren. She spends most of her time in her studio, where she designs and stitches quilts for books and fabric companies, plays on her longarm, and designs fabric. She loves to travel and teach quilt classes, and her students always take away inspiration and confidence for the tasks ahead.

Quilting since 1993, Cheryl loves all aspects of quilting, except the handwork, and with determination will find a way to do almost everything by machine. She started designing quilts in 1998 for her pattern company, cheryl rose creations, and this is her fifth book with C&T Publishing.

For more information on her lectures and workshops, for a peek into what's going on in her life, or to contact her, visit her website at www.cherylmalkowski.com or her blog at www.cherylmalkowski.com/blog. You can also follow her on Facebook at www.facebook.com/cherylmalkowski.quilting.

Other books by author:

Available in print only

For a list of other fine books from C&T Publishing, visit our website to view our catalog online.

C&T PUBLISHING, INC.
P.O. Box 1456
Lafayette, CA 94549
800-284-1114
Email: ctinfo@ctpub.com
Website: www.ctpub.com

C&T Publishing's professional photography services are now available to the public. Visit us at www.ctmediaservices.com.

Tips and Techniques can be found at www.ctpub.com > Consumer Resources > Quiltmaking Basics: Tips & Techniques for Quiltmaking & More

For quilting supplies:

COTTON PATCH
1025 Brown Ave.
Lafayette, CA 94549
Store: 925-284-1177
Mail order: 925-283-7883
Email: CottonPa@aol.com
Website: www.quiltusa.com

Note: Fabrics shown may not be currently available, as fabric manufacturers keep most fabrics in print for only a short time.